The Idea of Race
in Latin America, 1870–1940

iLAS *Critical Reflections on Latin America Series*

Institute of Latin American Studies
University of Texas at Austin

THE IDEA OF RACE
IN LATIN AMERICA, 1870–1940

Edited and with an Introduction by RICHARD GRAHAM
With chapters by
THOMAS E. SKIDMORE, ALINE HELG
and ALAN KNIGHT

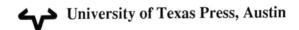 University of Texas Press, Austin

Seventh paperback printing, 2004

Requests for permission to reproduce material from this work should be sent to:

Permissions
University of Texas Press
P.O. Box 7819
Austin, Texas 78713-7819

⊗ The paper used in this publication meets the minimum requirements of
American National Standard for Information Sciences—Permanence of
Paper for Printed Library Materials, ANSI Z39.48–1984.

Library of Congress Cataloging-in-Publication Data

The Idea of Race in Latin America, 1870–1940 / edited and with an
    introduction by Richard Graham ; with chapters by Thomas E.
    Skidmore, Aline Helg, and Alan Knight.
        p.   cm. — (Critical reflections on Latin America series)
    Includes bibliographical references.
    ISBN 0-292-73857-9 (pbk.)
    1. Race. 2. Latin America — Race relations. 3. Latin America
—Politics and government — 1830–1948.   I. Graham, Richard, 1934–
II. Skidmore, Thomas E. III. Helg, Aline, 1953–   . IV. Knight,
Alan, 1946–   . V. Series.
HT1521.I34   1990
305.8′0098—dc20   89-39614

Contents

Preface

The origins of these studies are to be found in 1986 when Dr. Aline Helg arrived at the University of Texas at Austin from the University of Geneva. Financed by a three-year Swiss National Research Fellowship, she had decided to use this campus as a base for her research on race relations and the idea of race in Latin America. Her presence served as a catalyst in the creation of a loosely organized on-campus workshop to examine racialist ideas over time and in many places. Participants included Professors Robert Abzug, Davis Bowman, Richard Graham, Armando Gutierrez, Aline Helg, Bruce Hunt, Alan Knight, Henry Selby, and George Wright. At one point we invited several scholars from off campus to join us in a two-day session. Those scholars were Albert Camarillo, Moisés González Navarro, Charles A. Hale, John S. Haller, Jr., Nathan Huggins, Nancy Stepan, and Sheila Weiss. In making that mini-conference a reality we received support from Robert F. King (Dean, Liberal Arts), Bryan Roberts (Director, Center for Mexican Studies), Standish Meacham (Chairman, Department of History), Rodolfo de la Garza (Director, Mexican-American Studies), and George Wright (Director, Afro-American Studies). I take pleasure in gratefully acknowledging that support. Out of that workshop emerged the idea of a small book that would address the idea of race in Latin America to be included in the series "Critical Reflections on Latin America" published by the Institute of Latin American Studies.

A word on the contributors: Thomas Skidmore is the Cespedes Professor of Latin American History at Brown University. In addition to two major books on the politics of Brazil since 1930, he is the author of *Black into White: Race and Nationality in Brazilian Thought* (1974). Aline Helg is Assistant Professor of History, the University of Texas at Austin. She is the author of *Civiliser le peuple et former les élites: l'educatión en Colombie, 1918–1957* (1984), translated and published in Colombia in 1987 as *La educación en Colombia, 1918–1957: una historia social, economica y politica.* Alan Knight is the Annabel Irion Worsham Centennial Professor of History, University of Texas at Austin. He is the author of *The Mexican Revolution* (1986). Their patience and cooperation as we have moved this project to concrete reality are much appreciated; their intellectual contribution and the excitement they brought with them made my work a pleasure.—R.G.

1. Introduction

RICHARD GRAHAM

The racial theories prevailing in European, North American, and Latin American thought from the mid-nineteenth century until the 1920s (and even to 1945) decidedly shaped public policies on a number of important issues. Initiated in Europe, the classification and ranking of humankind into inferior and superior races profoundly influenced the development, indeed, the very creation of the sciences. Biology, medicine, psychology, anthropology, ethnology, and sociology were all to some degree shaped by an evolutionary paradigm. The spread of European colonialism and the rapid growth of the United States in the latter half of the nineteenth century brought additional and supposedly irrefutable proof of the validity of a scheme that placed the so-called primitive African or Indian at the bottom of the scale and at its top the "civilized" white European. Many social policies regarding education, crime, health, and immigration were informed by these dominant racial theories. Although the racialist conception of human beings began to lose its credibility from the early twentieth century, it was not until the Nazis began to apply those concepts to eugenics and to undertake massive extermination of the "inferior" races that most scientists firmly denounced the, by then, pseudo-scientific character of racial theories.

It is now a commonplace among historians to refer to hegemonic ideologies through which, it is argued, dominant classes shape the entire culture of their society, creating the predominant intellectual categories and limiting the possible range of any challenge. These ideologies are accepted (at least for awhile) by the very groups who are thereby controlled. The idea of race as it was formulated in the nineteenth century seems to have served that function both within particular countries and in maintaining or at least in justifying the economic and political power exercised by some nations over others. Within colonial and neo-colonial regions of the world it often legitimated rule by the metropolis. The idea of race also made it possible, paradoxically, for mestizos and mulattoes—by identifying themselves with white elites as against Indian or black majorities—to accept theories that justified white domination over "colored" populations. It is to explore some aspects of this process within Latin America that the chapters of this book have been assembled.

The period chosen for study, running more or less from 1870 to 1940, was the one in which the idea of race had its fullest development and received the imprimatur of science. To be sure, the belief in the superiority of one human group over another—groups that were often defined somatically—is perhaps as old as humankind itself. In European thought the identification of Africans with inferiority was already common at the time of the Renaissance. With the discovery of America, an intense debate erupted regarding the nature of the Amerindians; but the practice of subjugating them soon overrode any theoretical objections. Eighteenth-century developments in science and the continuing spread of a world economic system centered on northern Europe stimulated the impulse toward classifying all people according to some sort of scientific schema. That tendency is apparent in Carl von Linnaeus' *Systema naturae* (10th ed., 1758), and Johann Friedrich Blumenbach, *De generis humani varietate nativa* (1775)—who coined the word "Caucasian." But it was the work of Charles Darwin or, more exactly, interpretations and extensions by others of his *The Origin of the Species* (1859) and, especially, his *The Descent of Man* (1871) that established a supposed scientific basis for racism.[1]

As a successful propagandist of the new truth, no one exceeded Herbert Spencer (1820–1903). He was unmistakably the most imaginative nineteenth-century thinker to apply Darwin's theory to human society. He first named that theory "evolution," first used the phrase "survival of the fittest," and firmly linked biology to the idea of progress, so powerfully attractive at that time: "Evolution can end only in the establishment of the greatest perfection and most complete happiness." Human societies, he argued, developed according to the same rules of differentiation and organization as did living organisms, and, as society "grows, its parts become unlike: it exhibits increase of structure." Or again, "The change from the homogeneous to the heterogeneous is displayed in the progress of civilization as a whole, as well as in the progress of every nation." It followed that natural selection and the survival of the fittest were inevitably the guiding principles both within particular societies and of race relations generally. Just as in the animal world "the struggle for existence has been an indispensable means to evolution," just so with "social organisms." And differing races exhibited differential abilities to survive and dominate, so that some were destined to triumph over others.[2] Other popularizers of what has come to be called "Social Darwinism" did not delay in appearing, but its spread in Latin America may be largely ascribed to the influence of Spencer.[3]

Latin Americans faced a difficult intellectual dilemma regarding race. On the one hand, racial heterogeneity characterized most of their societies. On the other, many Latin Americans aspired to an ever closer connection to Europe and sought to follow its leadership in every realm. From the time most of their countries gained political independence from Spain and Portugal in the early nineteenth century, Latin American elites strove for an ever closer integration with the northern European system, whether in trade or in finance, whether in politics or intellectual life. As the expanding forces of industrial capitalism penetrated ever deeper into the Latin American economies, so did accompanying social change and intellectual currents.

Political and intellectual leaders imagined themselves part of a European civilization. Nineteenth-century liberalism—which also had an overpowering influence upon their thought—emphasized the idea of the free individual struggling to survive and ascend.[4] Scientific racism explained why some succeeded while others failed, seemed to make clear the reasons for contemporary realities in international relations, and justified the dominance domestically of the few (whites) over the many (colored). As the technological achievements of Europeans and North Americans clearly rested on science, its dictums took on a particular prestige. And the most eminent scientists then endorsed the view that the white race was superior and destined to triumph over blacks, Indians, mestizos, and mulattoes. Yet, with the mixed and varied racial composition of their societies clearly before them and a growing sense of national identity impelling consideration of national futures, these leaders also hesitated. What to believe? What to do?

Their sometimes anguished response forms the subject of this book. Some accepted European racist theory without question. Others picked and chose according to what seemed to fit reality as they knew it. As Thomas Skidmore points out, Brazilian intellectuals ignored the "scientific" condemnation of race mixture and spoke instead of how Brazil would move toward progress through a steady "whitening" of its population. They simply ignored the fact that such a process must inevitably imply a "darkening" of some. Race, for them, was not immutable, and Brazil, far from being condemned to subservience, was destined for a bright future—only a bit later, after the continuous process of race mixture along with immigration from Europe and the alleged reproductive weakness of blacks had had time to work their magic. Similarly for Argentinean and Cuban thinkers, as Aline Helg shows, whitening offered an escape from the cul de sac posed by European theories of race. Yet in Argentina, where blacks had already seemed to disappear through race mixture and where Indians had been ruthlessly exterminated, it was possible to believe more wholeheartedly in scientific racism (without sacrificing nationalist hopes) than was the case in Brazil and Cuba. But even Argentines chose from the writings of Europeans what they wanted to believe and did not focus their attention on the alleged racial differences among Europeans themselves, differences that would have placed Italians, Spaniards, and their descendants at a competetive disadvantage vis-à-vis "Aryans."

Even those who later ostensibly opposed scientific racism accepted many of its premises, sometimes unconsciously. Alan Knight shows that in Mexico, where the Revolution of 1910 wrought so many drastic changes, political and intellectual elites set themselves the task of opposing the racist philosophy that had played so important a part in the discourse of the prerevolutionary regime. Yet these spokesmen for *indigenismo* more often than not failed to distinguish between race and ethnicity, often revealed a reverse racism every bit as intellectually flawed as that of those whom they opposed, and allowed anti-Chinese racism to flourish without criticism. Similarly, the Brazilian race-theories critic Gilberto Freyre fell back upon categories of thought initially formulated by those whom he attacked.

The mestizo and mulatto played an important part in the thinking both of racists and antiracists in Mexico, Brazil, and Cuba. José Vasconcelos, the Mexican philosopher, was only one of the writers, albeit the most eloquent one, to claim the mestizo as the apotheosis of human development. Freyre hailed race mixture as a national achievement for which Brazil should be proud. For all of these writers, genetically inherited characteristics continued to play a role inconsistent with a nonracist approach.

Everywhere, racialist thinking impelled policy decisions. In Argentina, Brazil, and Cuba (and in Mexico before 1910) it directly affected immigration laws. In Brazil and Cuba it was used to defend particular responses to criminal behavior. In Cuba it shaped policies toward "witchcraft," encouraged even some segregationist policies, affected legislation regarding elections, and fostered the bloody repression of a black political party. Argentine reaction to labor unrest was guided by a belief in the danger posed by Russian Jews because of their race. Prerevolutionary Mexico had drawn on racialist theories to justify the disappropriation of Indian communities, as well as a particular model of economic development and project for nation building. Mexican revolutionaries similarly drew on concepts about race to rationalize policies designed to advance the state while encouraging the formation of national consciousness. And everywhere in Latin America thinkers understood education to be a possible escape from racialist determinism, even as they partly accepted that determinism.

In all four countries a close link existed between racism and reform. It was José Ingenieros, who so vibrantly called for restructuring the Argentine university curriculum and the destruction of the outdated Spanish colonial educational system, who led in the advocacy of racist philosophies. It was Fernando Ortiz in Cuba and Nina Rodrigues in Brazil, pioneer students of Afro–Latin American culture, who endorsed the idea of innate black criminality. At first it was liberal reformers who provided the intellectual and political context for the introduction and acceptance of social Darwinism. Later, in the Mexican case especially, it was revolutionaries and reformers who perpetuated stereotypes and labels that justified or rationalized the treatment of Indians as objects of state intervention rather than historical actors in their own right. It is the tension between a racially complex reality all about them and the supposed logic of their thought that makes the idea of race in Latin America a particularly fascinating subject.

Notes

1. Winthrop P. Jordan, *White over Black: American Attitudes toward the Negro, 1550–1812* (1968; reprint New York: Norton, 1977), pp. 3–43; Lewis Hanke, *Aristotle and the American Indians: A Study in Race Prejudice in the Modern World* (London: Hollis & Carter, 1959); [M. F.] Ashley Montagu, *Man's Most Dangerous Myth* (New York: Columbia University Press, 1942), pp. 3–36; idem, *The Idea of Race* (Lincoln: University of Nebraska Press, 1965); John S. Haller, Jr., *Outcasts*

from Evolution: Scientific Attitudes of Racial Inferiority, 1859–1900 (Urbana: University of Illinois Press, 1971), pp. 3–6; Nancy Stepan, *The Idea of Race in Science: Great Britain, 1800–1960* (London: Macmillan in Association with St. Antony's College, Oxford, 1982), pp. 1–110; Stephen Jay Gould, *Ever Since Darwin: Reflections in Natural History* (New York: Norton, 1977). A useful account of the trajectory of the idea of race is to be found in Michael Banton, *Racial Theories* (Cambridge, England: Cambridge University Press, 1987).

2. Herbert Spencer, *First Principles*, [? ed.] (New York: Appleton, 1898), p. 530; idem, *The Principles of Sociology*, 3 vols. (New York: Appleton, 1889), I: 462 and II: 241; idem, "Progress: Its Law and Cause," in *Essays, Scientific, Political and Speculative*, 3 vols. (New York: Appleton, 1891), I: 19.

3. His influence was also great in North America; see Richard Hofstadter, *Social Darwinism in American Thought, 1860–1915* (Philadelphia: University of Pennsylvania Press, 1944). On the spread of Darwin's science see Thomas F. Glick, ed., *The Comparative Reception of Darwinism* (Austin: University of Texas Press, 1974). Among other authors, Joseph Arthur de Gobineau had a particularly strong influence in Latin America.

4. See the masterful summary of the period's intellectual currents by Charles A. Hale, "Political and Social Ideas in Latin America, 1870–1930," in *The Cambridge History of Latin America*, ed. Leslie Bethell, vol. 4 (Cambridge: Cambridge University Press, 1988), pp. 367–414.

2. Racial Ideas and Social Policy in Brazil, 1870–1940

THOMAS E. SKIDMORE

Brazil received more African slaves than any other country in the Americas. Its legacy is one of the most interesting but often misunderstood multiracial societies in the world. Unlike the United States, which has a largely biracial structure, Brazil has long had a large mixed-race intermediate category, which one U.S. historian has seen as the key (the "mulatto escape hatch") to understanding present-day Brazilian race relations.[1] But how have the Brazilians seen the racial dimension of their society? This chapter offers an analysis of the intellectual and political elite's predominant racial ideas and attendant social policies from 1870—when final abolition of slavery (1888) was still nearly two decades away—until 1940, when scientific racism had lost its sway but Brazil had not yet found an accurate way to describe and debate its race relations.[2]

The Whitening Ideal

Thought about race in 1870 is best understood as it related to the predominant social ideology. The relationship is twofold. First, Brazilian thinkers worried about their past—they asked themselves whether heavy miscegenation and the resulting racially mixed population had predestined them to perpetual third-class status as a nation. If so, then they were caught in a determinist trap. Little could be done except to understand how their ethnic formation had doomed them. If, however, the future left room for maneuver, if ethnic "redemption" were somehow possible, then social policies might be devised to accelerate national development through economic modernization. The latter possibility raised the second question: How should they prepare for the future? How, in other words, should the country manage its resources for national development?

After 1870 the Brazilian elite came to accept an identifiable ideology of development. It was a form of classic liberalism—calling for secularization of the state (schools, marriage, cemeteries), the abolition of all restraints on individual freedom, as well as the decentralization of government.[3] The most obvious restraint on freedom was slavery. Thus the predominant ideology could focus on the single issue of legal servitude. As a result, the elite thought more about slavery than about either color or race. And since total abolition took so long—until 1888—this fixation on slavery per se gained, quite understandably, a very strong hold on the liberal mind. Nonetheless, the abolitionist liberals—who undoubtedly included the majority of the (few) "intellectuals" by the 1880s—did have some interesting views on race.

Before examining those views, we should remind ourselves of the actual social structure in Brazil in 1870. Most important, there already existed a large number of free Afro-Brazilians—mostly mulatto but also black. Scholars disagree over how these persons were able to become free—Gilberto Freyre (to be discussed in detail below) and Frank Tannenbaum have emphasized the institutional and cultural factors, such as the previous Iberian experience with dark peoples and the intervening power of the church and crown, which allegedly prevented the total dehumanization of the slave and thus encouraged manumission.[4] Others, such as Marvin Harris, stress the demographic context, arguing that the relative shortage of whites left the planter class no choice but to allow and even facilitate the emergence of a free class of mixed bloods to serve as artisans and cattle herders. In other words, Brazil had economic "space" for free persons of color—unlike most of the American South, where poor whites preempted these positions.[5]

Whatever the explanation, by 1870 Brazil had a significant percentage of free Afro-Brazilians throughout the country. Neither race nor slavery could be seen as a strictly regional problem, nor could one merely speculate about any "new" problem posed by free Afro-Brazilians after abolition—they had already won access (if only on a very small scale) to the highest reaches of society. Mulattoes such as the Baron of Cotegipe (an outstanding Conservative prime minister) and André Rebouças (a famous engineer of the empire), showed how far one could go. The census of 1872 listed only 38 percent of the population as "white." Twenty percent were listed as "black" and the remainder were classified as mulatto ("pardo" in the Brazilian taxonomy).[6]

What, then, did the Brazilian intellectual and political elite think about race between 1870 and 1888? These were the years when the liberal ideology rapidly conquered the younger generation. The culmination of its influence came with the abolition of slavery in 1888, the establishment of a republic in 1889, and the rapid realization between 1889 and 1892 of such liberal goals as disestablishment of the church, secularization of the schools and cemeteries, institution of civil marriage, and decentralization of government. In this atmosphere of liberal agitation, race was seldom discussed per se; instead, liberals talked about slavery. In their writings, however, one can find the following strands of thought:[7]

(1) Virtually no one believed in the simple theory of biological inferiority, so abolitionists only rarely tried to refute racist doctrines. Even the defenders of slavery argued that it was a necessary evil in order to maintain the economy—and they always added that Brazilian slaves were physically better off than many free workers in Europe. Occasionally, the opponents of abolition cast doubt on the humanity of the Afro-Brazilian slave. Exceedingly seldom did they go so far as to claim that Afro-Brazilians were biologically fated to perpetual servitude.[8]

(2) Abolitionists did worry about the large, illiterate, unskilled mass represented by the slaves. Few of them, however, thought through the probable social consequences of abolition. How would ex-slaves be employed? How could they be trained and prepared for a free life? Where would they go? André Rebouças, the mulatto engineer and abolitionist leader, was an exception—as early as 1883 he outlined a plan for modernization in agriculture that would streamline the commercial sector.[9] The majority of liberal abolitionists, however, preferred to think about European immigrants as the solution to the postabolition labor problem. Throughout the speeches and writings of such prominent abolitionists as Joaquim Nabuco and José do Patrocínio one finds this logic: we must abolish slavery because its continued existence repels potential European immigrants, whom we badly need.[10]

(3) Abolitionists believed that miscegenation would gradually and inexorably "whiten" and thereby "upgrade" the Brazilian population. This view can be found quite clearly in both Joaquim Nabuco and José do Patrocínio.[11]

It is at this point that the Brazilian view of race becomes complicated and interesting. Having rejected the straightforward theory of absolute biological differences, the abolitionists nonetheless believed in racial influences. Those relative influences were hardly a matter of indifference. The abolitionists, like most of the elite, hoped to maximize the influence of the "higher" or "more advanced" civilization—meaning the white European. Ergo: the whiter the better. Occasionally this concept of whitening could be read in cultural, not physiological, terms, for example, the famous incident related by Henry Koster when he asked in 1816 about the royal officer who looked dark—"Can a *capitão-mor* be a mulatto?" was his host's reply.[12] Here color attributed to an individual became a function of his social position. Yet even this interpretation meant that the darker persons had to whiten culturally—an enormous task. How could it be done? By maximizing their contact with individuals who were more advanced culturally. One of the easiest channels was intermarriage. Miscegenation, therefore, was seen as regenerative, if not biologically, at least in terms of culture contacts.

A case in point was the reaction by abolitionists to the proposal for importing Chinese coolies into Brazil in 1879. Planters (and even republicans such as Salvador de Mendonça) saw coolies as a ready replacement for the slaves whose attrition had become inevitable with the end of the slave trade in 1850 and the law of free birth in 1871. Joaquim Nabuco, the leading abolitionist politician of the day, vigorously opposed the coolie proposal on the grounds that Brazil already had enough trouble balancing off its African Blood without importing Asian Blood![13]

The whitening thesis got unique support in Brazil from the widespread belief, later popularized by Gilberto Freyre, that the Portuguese enjoyed an uncanny ability to whiten the darker peoples with whom they mixed. At times, this view seemed almost to amount to a faith in the "strong" genes of the amorous Portuguese. Underlying the belief was a largely unverified conclusion that black and mulatto net reproduction was low. Often this phenomenon was attributed to allegedly low fertility among blacks or mulattoes. In any case, it was taken as comforting proof that Brazil's color problem would gradually and inevitably disappear. As European immigrants increased the white element, the darker strain would naturally fade, either through miscegenation or through failure to reproduce.

How can one summarize thought about the Afro-Brazilian before 1888? The abolitionists believed that slavery was a moral, economic, and political drag on the nation's development. They saw the heritage of slavery as a mass of passive "premodern" workers who could, in their present state, contribute little to the rapid development of Brazil. The immediate solution was to import Europeans, thereby increasing the "white" (sometimes defined in cultural terms) element. The purely black element was fated to disappear, as the Brazilian population steadily whitened.

The history of Brazilian thought about race changed sharply after total abolition was achieved in 1888. At this point intellectual influences from abroad affected the country in a manner very different from the era of the abolitionist campaign. The nineteenth century had witnessed two contradictory movements of thought about race. On the one hand, the antislavery movement triumphed throughout the North Atlantic basin and finally even in the South Atlantic. While slavery crumbled under the impact of economic change and moral pressure, however, European thinkers were articulating systematic theories of innate biological differences among races. After Wilberforce came Gobineau.

Brazil was slower to pick up the currents of European thought than some of its Latin American neighbors. The absence of universities helped maintain its relative isolation. The growth and apparent victory of the liberal cosmopolitan ideology in the 1880s, however, signaled an intensified interest in the latest European ideas. Brazil was very vulnerable, like the rest of Latin America, to European theories of race. Ironically, the two decades after total abolition were a high period for theories of biological inferiority and superiority.

Furthermore, Brazilians now had to focus on race, not slavery. Many of the questions that could be avoided or glossed over before 1888 came to the fore. And the harder Brazilian intellectuals tried to inform themselves about the latest ideas from Europe—for them the citadel of culture and progress—the more they heard about the inherent inferiority of the black. In France, for example, the imposing historical theories of Arthur de Gobineau were supported by the "scientific" anthropology and anthropogeography of Gustave Le Bon and Georges Vacher de Lapouge.[14]

Brazilian social thinkers now faced a difficult task: How could they evaluate the "scientific" race theories being imported from Europe and, to a lesser extent, from North America? The anthropological theories, which even went to the point of "proving" Aryan superiority by measuring cranial capacity, were reinforced by the social-Darwinist doctrines dominant in England and the United States. Because of their inherent biological inferiority, so the reasoning went, darker races were bound to be dominated, and perhaps even eliminated, by the "stronger" Aryans. Like the dinosaur, the black could not argue with evolution, as the struggle now took on a social as well as a strictly physiological form.

The influence of these theories was great in Brazil, at least among prominent writers. The black became a target for study, a laboratory subject. Nina Rodrigues, for example, the acknowledged pioneer in this field, attempted to catalogue African social customs as they had been transmitted to Brazil by the slaves. In addition to this seemingly neutral exercise, however, he also studied the social behavior of blacks and mixed bloods in the light of Lombrosian theory. Criminal tendencies among blacks, for example, were explained by analyzing their skulls. His approach to criminal medicine—which clearly followed dominant European theories—greatly influenced the succeeding generation of anthropologists and sociologists (such as Afrânio Peixoto and Arthur Ramos). Rodrigues held the chair of legal medicine in the Bahia Medical Faculty from 1891 until 1905. To appreciate how far he carried Lombrosian theory, one need only remember that he recommended different treatment of convicted criminals according to their race. Furthermore, his racially based theory of collective hysteria—applied to the famous case of the messianic Antônio Conselheiro and his millenarian followers in Canudos—greatly influenced Euclides da Cunha, the man who immortalized them in his *Rebellion in the Backlands*.[15]

Euclides is himself an interesting case study. He was the personification of the self-taught Brazilian intellectual desperately attempting to keep up with the latest developments in European social science. Among the European thinkers he absorbed secondhand (through his faithful intermediary Francisco Escobar) was the Polish racist theoretician Ludwig Gumplowicz. Euclides managed at times to shake off determinist thoughts about the *caboclo*, who resulted from Euro-Indian unions. Euclides saw the *caboclo* as the backbone of a new race uniquely adapted to the rigors of the harsh interior of the Brazilian Northeast. But the black and the mulatto got no such reprieve. Euclides regarded them, especially the mulatto, as degenerates.[16]

It is hardly surprising that Brazilian intellectuals picked up racist ideas from abroad. Books by European racists such as Le Bon were widely used in Brazilian schools. Visiting European lecturers such as James Bryce openly lamented Brazil's "plight"—a huge black and mestizo population.[17] Innumerable visitors from North America and Europe reinforced, through their comments, the pseudo-scientific racist writings dominant in their countries. During these years Brazilian intellectuals experienced an intense feeling of inferiority vis-à-vis Europe and the United States.

Could it be that the intellectuals, insecure in their modest outpost of European culture, were repeating European ideas that in fact did not significantly influence Brazilian social customs? It is certainly true that many members of the Brazilian intellectual and political elite were consciously catering to European prejudices in order to win the capital and immigrants they believed indispensable for Brazil's development. In attempting to refute European prejudices against the tropical climate, Brazilian propagandists had an easier task: they could simply point to relatively temperate southern Brazil, where levels of disease and temperature were equivalent to those in Europe, especially Italy. But in the case of race, it was difficult. Usually the black or mulatto was simply not mentioned in propaganda aimed at potential immigrants. This omission was practiced symbolically by Baron Rio Branco, Brazil's foreign minister from 1902 to 1912, who was thoroughly familiar with European prejudices, because he had served his country abroad for thirty years. As foreign minister he followed a "white only" policy in recruiting diplomats and in choosing special envoys for missions abroad. He preferred the tall, handsome blond types, such as Joaquim Nabuco, who was appointed ambassador to Washington in 1902. Short men of apparently questionable ethnic origins, such as Euclides da Cunha, were less welcome; his missions for the Foreign Office were limited to border disputes in the Amazon Valley.[18]

Nor should this white only policy surprise us. Brazil was, after all, poorly prepared to argue with the powerful, racially conscious nations. Rio Branco, like other Brazilian leaders, knew well that his country was looked down on as an African potpourri by Argentines, who were far more successful, in relative terms, than Brazil in attracting European immigrants. Furthermore, Brazilians were ill-equipped intellectually to refute the supposedly scientific theories of race pouring out of Europe and North America. Whatever may have been their intuitions about their own experience as a racially mixed society, they found it difficult to defend antiracist doctrines against the weight of prestigious opinion abroad.

What were the other characteristics of Brazilian thought about race between 1888 and 1914? As might be expected, little practical attention was given to the actual situation of the ex-slave. Instead, attention focused on the immigrant. There was a certain logic, not necessarily racist, to this preference. Brazil needed skilled human capital. "Skilled" meant at least literate, and with some experience of a developed society. Immigrants, if available, were undoubtedly a cheaper source for such labor than the ex-slaves, whose basic education and training would prove more expensive, or at least, so it could have been argued.

But, seeking immigrants also fitted in with the continuation of the whitening ideology earlier predominant among the abolitionists. This was a subtle, often unarticulated ideology. Occasionally, it was stated openly. Such was the case when José Veríssimo, the noted literary critic, wrote, "I am convinced . . . that western civilization can only be the work of the white race, and that no great civilization can be built with mixed peoples. As ethnographers assure us . . . race mixture is facilitating the prevalence of the superior element. Sooner or later it will perforce eliminate the black race here. And . . . immigration . . . will, through the inevitable mixtures, accelerate the selection process."[19]

This whitening ideology, which accepted the mulatto but not the black, had one advantage for uneasy Brazilian intellectuals: it was a compromise with racist determinism. Instead of two exclusive ethnic categories, it presupposed a miraculous movement from black in the direction of white. Thus Brazil could slowly, thanks to the low net reproduction rate among blacks, work its way out of the determinist trap.

Raimundo Nina Rodrigues (1862–1906).
Photographer unknown, courtesy of
Companhia Editora Nacional, São Paulo,
Brazil.

Princess Isabel and the Count d'Eu cheered by the crowds after the signing of the Lei Aurea abolishing slavery on May 13, 1888. Photo courtesy of Gilberto Ferrez.

Basketmaker, Rio de Janeiro, 1895. Photo courtesy of Gilberto Ferrez.

Gilberto Freyre with freed slave. Photo courtesy of the
Nettie Lee Benson Latin American Collection, General
Libraries, University of Texas at Austin.

This was true, of course, only as long as one did not at the same time believe the current theories that condemned the racially mixed as degenerate. Fortunately for them, most thinkers simply ignored or glossed over this fatal objection. In other words, the whitening ideology was the Brazilian compromise. Obviously unable to claim white racial purity for any part of the country—unlike the North Americans—Brazilians seemed to accept the racist theory of Aryan (or at least white) superiority and then promptly escaped the seemingly determinist trap by implicitly denying the absoluteness of racial differences. The whiter the better. To my knowledge, there was no writer who was explicitly aware of the contradiction in this position. How could one accept absolute racial differences and then argue that the Brazilian population was moving gradually from inferior to superior? Such reasoning presupposed a shaded area that simply did not exist in rigorous racist thought.

As I have indicated above, many Brazilian intellectuals must have implicitly assented to racist ideas after 1888 without actually spelling them out. One proof of this is the manner in which the few courageous antiracist writers before 1914 in Brazil phrased their arguments. Writers such as Alberto Torres, Manuel Bomfim, Alvaro Bomilcar, and Gilberto Amado began by asserting that theories of black inferiority and white superiority were generally believed in Brazil.[20] They had no doubt that, whatever Brazil's social behavior, the elite had swallowed racist ideas from Europe and North America. Having admitted this, they all took virtually the same way out of the determinist cul-de-sac: they explained history by emphasizing environment instead of race. Torres, for example (probably the most influential of the antiracists writing before 1914), cited the work of Franz Boas, later to be Gilberto Freyre's teacher, to prove that biological theories of race were being refuted by the most recent science.[21] Torres, like Bomfim, looked to history and the social habits ingrained historically to explain the relative backwardness of Brazil. Their views were often summed up in the phrase, "There are no inferior and superior races, only advanced and retarded races." The latter characterization was always explained to mean that there was no inherent reason why they could not catch up.[22]

But these critics of racism remained a minority before the First World War. It was not that they were directly countered by other writers expressing racist views. Rather, they were ignored or read skeptically. Nonetheless, they had an effect. They were pointing the way to an escape from the straitjacket of racism.

When did these critics begin to represent more than a small minority position among Brazilian intellectuals? I think it was during the First World War. The shift in opinion was connected with the undermining of the liberal cosmopolitan ideology that had emerged during the late Empire.[23] In the era of the Brazilian belle epoque, from 1900 to 1914, the ideology seemed to go unchallenged. Foreign capital was eagerly courted, and Brazilians dutifully listened to the racist views of distinguished visitors. At the same time, as we have seen, some isolated critics were attacking the dominant ideology, along with one of its principal corollaries—the theory of racial superiority.

How did acceptance of the criticism grow? In a manner that should not surprise us: antiracism became a tenet of the new nationalist thought. Alberto Torres and Alvaro Bomilcar were nationalist prophets. Torres thought he could establish a nationalist position only after he had effectively refuted the theory of white superiority. Thus it was an integral part of his overall nationalist attack on liberal cosmopolitanism. To realize this, one need only look at the way in which Torres correlated racist theory with the imperialist designs of the economically expansive powers. By impugning the human potential of nations such as Brazil, Torres explained, the industrial nations were attempting to justify—in both their own minds and those of the elite in the weaker nations—their economic penetration.[24]

Any nationalist thinker had to begin by defending the Brazilian, whom they all acknowledged to be beyond any hope of racial "purity." Alvaro Bomilcar is a good example. In 1911 he wrote a surprisingly forthright pamphlet called *O Preconceito de raça no Brasil* [Racial prejudice in Brazil], using the naval revolt of 1910 to show how widespread was discrimination against blacks (the enlisted ranks, almost entirely black in the navy, had rebelled to protest whipping!).[25] Bomilcar went on to help found the nationalist magazine *Brazilea* in 1917 and the Nativist Propaganda Association (Propaganda Nativista, which became the Ação Social Nacionalista in 1920). One of the group's nineteen basic tenets was "adoption of the principle of equality of the races."[26]

By 1918 one finds many more intellectuals openly contesting racist ideas. A minor essayist such as José Maria Belo in that year dismissed any explanation of Brazil's relative backwardness based on race or climate. "Fortunately," he noted, "all these pompous phrases . . . have gone out of fashion. Neither race nor climate has a decisive influence on the development of a country."[27] But Belo was overly optimistic. Intellectual styles in Brazil had not altered so quickly. Nonetheless, his comment was itself a sign of a major shift in elite opinion. After 1918 those who espoused racist theories were on the defensive. A younger generation, born with the Republic and abolition, was much more skeptical of racist theory from abroad. They looked to antiracist prophets such as Alberto Torres and Sílvio Romero for their inspiration, thereby finding Brazilian credentials for the antiracist theme in their nationalist thought.[28]

Here we need to remember that the Brazilian revolt against racist thought was directly related to the gradual discrediting of racist theories among European and North American scientists. Alberto Torres could quote Franz Boas and Bomilcar could quote Jean Finot. At worst, foreign scientific theory, if taken as a whole, was becoming contradictory and ambiguous. Thus the antiracist Brazilians could pick their own evidence to support refutations of the racists. Furthermore, the Brazilian elite was well aware of the fruits of systematic discrimination against the black in the United States. This U.S. practical application of racist thought offended even the more conservative Brazilians, whose personal experience made it impossible to accept such a dehumanizing and absolutistic system, especially when it came to the mulatto. Insofar, therefore, as Brazilian intellectuals connected North American social behavior with racist theory, they found the results morally and emotionally repugnant. When they looked at Europe it was easier to ignore the connection between theory and practice, because Western Europe had virtually no blacks or mulattoes. The war, however, helped undermine the prestige even of European thought and to dramatize the possible truth in charges by such Brazilians as Alberto Torres that racist thought was in fact an instrument used by industrialized countries to destroy the self-confidence of weaker, darker peoples whose natural resources they wished to plunder.

The 1920s and 1930s in Brazil saw a consolidation of the whitening ideal and its implicit acceptance by the idea makers and social critics. The doubts about race expressed by the elite in earlier years lost any tone of real conviction in this period. Interestingly, most writers did not come out and state unambiguously that race made no difference and that therefore the question should be ignored. Rather, they said that Brazil was progressively whitening, and therefore the problem was being solved. This is an important point. Certain scientists during the era were subscribing to the pure environmentalist hypothesis; some Brazilian writers were turning with enthusiasm to favorable treatments of the African heritage; and it is in this period that Gilberto Freyre made his reputation on optimistic interpretations of the national character that depended on a positive reinterpretation of the history of miscegenation in Brazil. At the same time (at the other end of the spectrum), German Nazism was reviving pure heredity arguments to indict Jews and blacks. The Brazilian elite steered its way between these positions. Political arguments about immigration and social criticism took place against the backdrop of the shared assumption that Brazilians were getting whiter and would continue to do so.

During the 1920s the whitening thesis received its most systematic statement from F. J. Oliveira Vianna, a lawyer-historian who became one of the most widely read interpreters of Brazilian reality between the wars. At first glance, Oliveira Vianna's ideas on race might have seemed a throwback. He made no effort to conceal his admiration for the masters of European racist thought, such as "the great Ratzel."[29] Yet, although he constantly referred to "inferior" and "superior" races, he did not regard such differences as absolute. This was, in fact, the compromise Brazilians had been making in order to reconcile racist theory and their multiracial reality. Inconsistent as it must have seemed to doctrinaire racists from Europe or North America, Vianna made degrees of inferiority the central concept in his interpretation of Brazil's racial evolution.

The Indigenous and the Afro-Brazilian were inexorably declining as a proportion of the population, he said. For evidence Vianna compared the racial proportions of the population in the 1872 and 1890 censuses.[30] In that period, the white proportion increased from 38 to 44 percent, while the black fell from nearly 20 percent to under 15 percent and the mixed *(mestiço)* fell from 38 to 32 percent (the Indian climbed from 4 percent to 9 percent).[31] Vianna's citing of these figures was all the more interesting in view of the fact that the 1920 census (for which his analysis was an introductory chapter) did not include any breakdown by race—an omission officially justified on the grounds that "the responses [on racial categories] largely hide the truth," although it may also have resulted from a desire (obviously shared by Vianna) to gloss over the degree to which Brazil was still nonwhite.[32] And he had a reassuring conclusion for the elite: immigration was playing the role Joaquim Nabuco had hoped.

Much of Vianna's favorable impact among the public must have come from those Brazilians who concentrated on the conclusion that Brazil was achieving ethnic purity by miscegenation and either were not bothered by the archaic terminology or chose to discount it as not undermining the validity of the conclusion.[33] In one sense, the contradiction between assumptions and conclusion was enormously reassuring: if an erudite scholar who knew and believed so much of the (increasingly less) prestigious scientific-racist theory from Europe and North America could conclude that Brazil's ethnic future was safe, then Brazilians could feel truly confident.

Vianna was thus an important transitional figure—bridging the gap between the scientific racism prevailing before 1914 and the environmentalist-social philosophy predominant after 1930. In both eras whitening was the elite's de facto racial goal. It was Vianna's explanation of the historical origins of that process that made his work so comprehensible to his readers.

As we have seen, only a few curious writers before 1930 devoted serious attention to the ethnography and sociology of the Africans and their Brazilian descendants.[34] Sílvio Romero made an impressive collection of Afro-Brazilian folklore for his pioneering history of Brazilian literature (first edition, 1888), although his example was not followed by any other major literary historian or critic. Nina Rodrigues, the Bahian medical professor of racist views, had begun an ambitious project of documenting Afro-Brazilian survivals in Bahia when death cut short his research in 1906.[35] In that same year the journalist João do Rio published a study of Afro-Brazilian religious customs in Rio de Janeiro. Finally, a doctor from Bahia, Manoel Querino, published a series of studies on Afro-Brazilian customs.[36] Aside from these pioneers, all relatively isolated in their labors and gaining little discussion of their findings, there was no serious interest in investigating or analyzing the African or Afro-Brazilian presence. Even these few investigators had no successors who published significantly until the 1930s.

The only other effective scientific exception to this pattern was the anthropologist Edgar Roquette-Pinto, whose work contributed to the development in Brazil of the rival theory of "culture," which was becoming by the 1920s in Europe and North America a keystone of environmentalist social science.[37] Like Euclides da Cunha, Roquette-Pinto was deeply troubled by the miserable condition of the people of the interior. Unlike Euclides, he soon came to question the racist assumptions of anthropogeography (Friedrich Ratzel et al.), which da Cunha never escaped. Although he never ceased to admire Euclides' courage as a pioneer amateur ethnographer who transformed his science into a literary work of universal appeal, by 1914 he had progressed far enough from Euclides' position to argue that, although much of the black population had been abandoned to "the kind of total ignorance that in the modern world makes man into a helpless biped," thus accelerating their disappearance, blacks (mulattoes were evidently excluded from this discussion) had, with proper education, shown themselves capable of great progress in the United States. Presumably, this could also happen in Brazil, although Roquette-Pinto ventured no prediction (significantly, he still cited Nina Rodrigues' research without any critical comment). By unequivocally rejecting the theory of mixed-blood degeneracy, Roquette-Pinto lent impressive scientific credentials to the growing campaign to rescue the native Brazilian from the determinist trap. Like Sílvio Romero, he thought that Brazil's greatest need was a realistic sense of confidence, thus avoiding both that "cruel defeatism that threatens to undermine the nation" and the "lazy optimism of those who hide to ward off danger."[38]

In the 1930s attention finally turned in a major way to the Afro-Brazilian heritage. A leader in the change was Arthur Ramos, a physician from Bahia. Ramos published a series of influential books and articles on Afro-Brazilian culture, drawing on materials collected by Nina Rodrigues, whose pioneering work Ramos greatly admired. Ramos added organizational ability to his research and teaching and was instrumental in founding the Brazilian Society of Anthropology and Ethnology in 1941.[39] He was also active in the Afro-Brazilian congresses held in Recife in 1934 and in Bahia in 1937.

Gilberto Freyre was another figure who contributed greatly to the study of the Afro-Brazilian and became a leading figure in the redefinition of Brazil's racial identity. He was a principal organizer of the first Afro-Brazilian Congress (1934) in Recife, his home city, where he had already established himself as the leader of a varied regionalist intellectual movement. Freyre's greatest impact came with the publication of *Casa grande e senzala* in 1933 (later translated into English as *The Masters and the Slaves*), a social history of the slave plantation world of Northeastern Brazil in the sixteenth and seventeenth centuries, when the sugar economy furnished the focus for Brazil's multiracial society.[40] Freyre's portrait, often impressionistic and idiosyncratic in its structure and documentation, provided a sympathetic insight into the intimate personal relations among the planter families and their slaves. In furnishing his detailed picture of this intensely patriarchical ethos, Freyre dwelt on the manifold ways in which the African and Afro-Brazilian deeply influenced the lifestyle of the planter class, in food, clothing, and sex. His first book was followed in 1936 by *Sobrados e mucambos* (translated as *The Mansions and the Shanties*)—a study of the urban-rural social conflux of the eighteenth and early nineteenth centuries that followed the same methodology and style.[41]

Casa grande e senzala turned on its head the question of whether generations of miscegenation had done irreparable damage.[42] Brazil's ethnic potpourri, Freyre argued, was an immense asset. He showed how research in nutrition, anthropology, medicine, psychology, sociology, and agronomy had rendered the racial theories obsolete and had pointed up new villains—insufficient diet, impractical clothing, and disease too often undiagnosed and untreated (especially syphilis). He quoted studies by Brazilian scientists, the product of a new and profound concern on the part of Brazilian intellectuals about the long-ignored social problems of their own country,[43] to show that the Indian and the Negro had made important contributions to a healthier diet and a more practical style of dress for Brazilians. Thus Freyre dramatized for a wider public the country's new knowledge of the racial dimensions of its own past.

Equally important for the book's popular success was the author's detailed description of the intimate social history of patriarchal society. While this approach incurred the criticism of a few academic critics abroad, it appealed to Brazilians because it helped explain the origin of their personalities.[44] At the same time, his readers were being given the first scholarly examination of Brazilian national character with an unabashedly optimistic message: Brazilians could be proud of their unique, ethnically mixed tropical civilization, whose social vices—which Freyre did not minimize—could be attributed primarily to the atmosphere of the slaveholding monoculture that dominated the country until the second half of the nineteenth century. The evil consequences of miscegenation stemmed not from race mixing itself, but from the unhealthy relationship of master and slave under which it occurred.[45]

Freyre's writings also did much to focus attention on the inherent value of Africans as the representatives of a high civilization in their own right. Freyre was thus furnishing, for those Brazilians who might want to take it that way, a rationale for a multiracial society in which the component "races"—European, African, and Indigenous—could be seen as *equally* valuable. The practical effect of his analysis was not, however, to promote such a racial egalitarianism. Rather, it served to reinforce the whitening ideal by showing graphically that the (primarily white) elite had gained valuable cultural traits from its intimate contact with the African (and Indigenous, to a lesser extent) component.

Other scholars also contributed, during the 1930s, to the exploration of the African and Afro-Brazilian contribution. Mário de Andrade, acknowledged leader of the modernist movement, studied the samba in São Paulo and folk festival images in Recife.[46] Edison Carneiro published extensively on the influence of African religion in Brazil.[47] Although many Brazilians must have read this kind of writing for its folkloric appeal, it nonetheless revealed a move away from the racist assumptions that dismissed the African as a barbarian of inferior stock.

A typical expression of the faith in whitening could be found in the prose of Fernando de Azevedo, a widely honored educational reformer who wrote the introduction to the census of 1940. His product, *A cultura brasileira* (first published in Brazil in 1943 and issued in an English translation in 1950), gained immediate acceptance as a standard interpretation of Brazilian civilization. The first chapter, on the role of land and race in Brazil, concluded with these words about the future:

> If we admit that blacks and Indians are continuing to disappear, and that immigration, especially that of a Mediterranean origin, is not at a standstill, the white man will not only have in Brazil his major field of life and culture in

the tropics, but be able to take from old Europe—citadel of the white race—before it passes to other hands, the torch of western civilization to which the Brazilians will give a new and intense light—that of the atmosphere of their own civilization.[48]

It was significant that Azevedo discussed Brazil's racial future on the occasion of a national census. Oliveira Vianna had given the first systematic exposition of his "Aryanization" theory in a chapter accompanying the census of 1920, although that document was conspicuous for not breaking down data by racial category. The census of 1940, which did include breakdown by race, provided evidence that Brazil's population was growing whiter, thereby furnishing support for the elite consensus that the African and Indigenous component would inexorably decline.

Immigration Policy

Although the public health campaigners, the scientific antiracists, and later the enthusiasts of Afro-Braziliana gave a new dimension to the debate over Brazil's ethnic future, the whitening ideal remained firmly entrenched among the political elite. It was clearly illustrated in the concern over immigration. In 1921 the western state of Mato Grosso made a land concession to developers. According to the press, these developers were linked to organizers in the United States who were recruiting black North Americans to emigrate to Brazil. The president of Mato Grosso (a Catholic bishop) immediately canceled the concession and so informed the Brazilian foreign minister; but the press continued to spread the alarm. As the eminent public health specialist Arthur Neiva wrote, "Why should Brazil, which has resolved its race problem so well, raise a question among us which has never even crossed our minds? Within a century the nation will be white."[49]

Two congressional deputies, Andrade Bezerra (from the northeastern state of Pernambuco) and Cincinnato Braga (São Paulo), thought strong action was needed and introduced a bill to prohibit entry into Brazil of "human beings of the black race." Its introduction provoked a heated debate in the lower house of the National Congress.[50] Several deputies branded it unconstitutional and therefore inadmissible for debate. Bezerra reminded his colleagues of the recent immigration laws in the United States, Canada, and Australia, "especially concerning those of Asian descent," and called for a "policy that will guard our national interests."

In 1923 Fidelis Reis, a federal deputy from Minas Gerais, introduced a slightly different version.[51] The color bar was now included in a larger proposal to expand the colonization service, which had been set up by the immigration law of 1907, but never effectively funded. Article five of the bill prohibited the entry of any colonists "of the black race" and limited Asians ("the yellow race") to an annual rate of no more than 3 percent of the Asians already resident in Brazil. (Quotas for immigrants had been incorporated in the National Origins Act passed in the United States in 1921.) Reis made specific reference to the U.S. law but noted that Brazil still had much greater need of European stock than its powerful northern neighbor. (It is interesting to note that even a spokesman who condemned black immigration stopped short of following in Brazil the implicit U.S. ethnic policy of discriminating among European immigrants.) Reis argued for stepping up the recruitment and systematic settlement of immigrants to meet " the constant complaint of landowners over the lack of labor." The African? Although he had "worked, suffered and with dedication helped us build this Brazil, it would have been better if we had never had him." Asians were almost as great a menace because their alleged failure to assimilate would guarantee the presence of "yellow cysts in the national organism," which would be as great a danger to Brazil as the concentration of Asians in California was to the United States.

Fidelis Reis was attacked by other deputies for his racism, as Bezerra and Braga had been. But his critics' comments showed how fully they shared his basic desire to see the population grow whiter. Several explained away the allegedly weak state of the population in the interior on the ground that they lacked proper health facilities, thereby showing the influence of the public health campaigns on their thinking. But even the apologists for the native-born Brazilians endorsed the idea that Brazil's ethnic problem was solving itself. The only way the bill's opponents really differed from Reis was in their assessment that the process was going well, while Reis thought the steady ascent toward whiteness seemed by no means assured (evidenced by his reference to the black as "an ever-present threat weighing down our destiny"). He saw the *mestiço* as an unreliable instrument for racial improvement and quoted Euclides da Cunha's famous passage on the instability of mixed bloods as proof. When other deputies expressed faith in the *mestiço* as the intermediary in the whitening process, he cited Louis Agassiz and Gustave LeBon as authorities for a contrary view.

An interesting division of opinion on the general question of color bars occurred among the ranks of delegates to the First Brazilian Congress of Eugenics in 1929. Azevedo Amaral, a prominent newspaper editor and strong advocate of the now increasingly anachronistic scientific-racist position, presented a ten-point program, which included a proposal to bar all nonwhite immigrants. The meeting took several votes, first defeating (by twenty to seventeen) a proposal to forbid all non-European immigrants, and then voting down the proposed baring of black immigrants by twenty-five to seventeen. The opposition to Amaral was led by Roquette-Pinto.[52]

What did these debates over immigration signify? First, it was still possible for respected politicians and intellectuals to propose color bars. Such a prohibition had, after all, been included in the immigration decree of 1891, although it did not appear in the Law of 1907. On the other hand, these bills were not passed, perhaps in part because there seemed so little real prospect of black immigrants coming from anywhere (including the United States). More important, most deputies, like most members of the elite, shied away from such overtly racist gestures as an absolute color bar. They believed in a whiter Brazil and thought they were getting there by a natural (almost miraculous?) process. An overt color bar smacked of the United

States, which remained a constant reminder of what all Brazilians considered an inhumane (and eventually self-defeating) solution to the ethnic problem. Why miscegenenation should have operated so benignly in Brazil and not in the United States (Brazilians often seemed to ignore the fact of extensive racial mixture in the United States) was seldom explained.

While the politicians and intellectuals debated, the government acted. In 1921 Brazilian consuls in the U.S. began, on Foreign Ministry orders, systematically refusing immigrant visas to U.S. black applicants. The U.S. State Department and the FBI actively collaborated in the policy, which was kept confidential by Brazilian authorities. Both governments apparently wanted to forestall the rise of black militancy and both feared, with some reason, that black migration might fuel it. The policy was ironical, since the blacks had been attracted to Brazil by its reputation for harmonious race relations—enthusiastically endorsed by prominent U.S. black visitors—and by its repeated appeals for immigrants. It was the strongly positive response of would-be U.S. black promoters of migration to Brazil that had frightened the Brazilian government into action.[53]

In 1934 a nationally elected Constituent Assembly gathered to frame a new constitution. After the Revolution of 1930 the provisional government of Getúlio Vargas had swept aside the Constitution of 1891 and ruled by decree. The provisional government had promised to call a Constituent Assembly, which finally met and drafted what became the Constitution of 1934. Article 121, Section 6, incorporated the principle of national quotas, which had been urged by Deputies Andrade Bezerra and Cincinnato Braga in the 1920s. The article read, "The entry of immigrants into the national territory will be subject to the restrictions necessary to guarantee the ethnic integration and the physical and legal capacity of the immigrant; the immigrant arrivals from any country cannot, however, exceed an annual rate of two percent of the total number of that nationality resident in Brazil during the preceding fifty years."[54] While debating this article, which was approved and included in the Constitution of 1934, congressmen said much about the need to avoid endangering the steady process of assimilation of all residents into a unified society. In fact, the restriction was aimed at the Japanese, who had been arriving since 1908 and against whose alleged resistance to assimilation a major campaign had been waged for over a decade.[55]

The same nationality quotas for immigrants were specified in the authoritarian Constitution of 1937 (Article 151), which Getúlio Vargas proclaimed after his coup in November of that year. Just before Vargas was deposed by the military in October 1945, his government issued an important decree-law (No. 7967 of September 18, 1945) stipulating that immigrants should be admitted in conformance with "the necessity to preserve and develop, in the ethnic composition of the population, the more desirable characteristics of its European ancestry." The framers of the Constitution of 1946, committed to the redemocratization of Brazil, conspicuously avoided putting any specifics on immigration into article 162, specifying instead that it would be regulated by law. Since no new body of immigration laws has ever been passed, Brazil has continued to live under the regulations with all their racist assumptions—laid down before 1946.[56]

Brazilian Reaction to Nazism: A Digression

The 1930s also brought news of a new source of racist thought—Hitler's Germany—that suggested racist ideas were not as dead as recent intellectual trends in Brazil might indicate. Brazil actually had its own rightist political movement, which bore some disturbing resemblances to European fascist parties. The Integralists (Ação Integralista Brasileira) became the fastest-growing Brazilian party after its founding in 1932.[57] Although its official documents never made racism a central theme, one prominent Integralist, Gustavo Barroso, advocated a virulently anti-Semitic line in numerous books and articles,[58] and the Integralist press reprinted Nazi propaganda against Jews. Brazilian authorities worried that the sizable German-speaking and Italian-speaking minorities in Brazil might listen receptively to the propaganda directed at them by the Mussolini and Hitler regimes, and in 1938 the Vargas government suppressed Nazi activities in Brazil, which had been extensive in the southern states where German settlement was heavy.[59] In fact, however, the great majority of foreign-born Brazilians and their children maintained their loyalty to their adopted country. Although some German-born showed interest in the Nazi movement, no significant number wanted to apply political racism in Brazil.[60]

Indeed Nazism provoked a sharp response from the new generation of Brazilian intellectuals. Twelve well-known writers, including Roquette-Pinto, Arthur Ramos, and Gilberto Freyre, were worried enough by October 1935 to issue the "Manifesto against Racial Prejudice,"warning that "transplanting of racist ideas and especially of their social and political correlates" was especially dangerous for a country like Brazil, "whose ethnic formation is extremely heterogeneous."

An even stronger manifesto was issued by the Brazilian Society of Anthropology and Ethnology in 1942.[61] It explicitly endorsed environmentalism (the 1935 manifesto was more cautious on that point), arguing that "anthropology furnishes no scientific basis for discriminatory acts against any people on the basis of supposed racial inferiority." It also cited other recent antiracist manifestoes, such as those of the biologists at the Seventh International Genetics Conference in Edinburgh in 1939 and of the American Anthropological Association in 1938, and included this claim for their country's unique success in the field of race relations:

> People of Indian, European, and African origins have mixed in an atmosphere of such liberality and such a complete absence of legal restrictions on miscegenation that Brazil has become the ideal land for a true community of people representing very diverse ethnic origins. . . . This Brazilian philosophy on the treatment of races is the best weapon we can offer against the monstrous Nazi philosophy, which is murdering and pillaging in the name of race . . .

These words were not always followed in practice. The discrepancy was clearest, as always, in immigration policy. Oswaldo Aranha, while foreign minister during the Vargas dictatorship (1937–1945), issued directives barring the immigration of European Jews, who were desperately attempting to escape the hand of Nazism. His logic was the same as that used in immigration policy in general: Brazil must restrict immigration to those who "identify with the Brazilian ethos" and exclude "types strange to the national organism, such as Jews *[israelitas]* and Japanese."[62] This anti-Semitic visa policy was not publicly acknowledged, just as the anti-black visa policy of the 1920s had not been. Once again it was in immigration policy that the Brazilian elite's racial fears were acted out.

Epilogue: Whitening—An Anachronistic Racial Ideal?

I have traced the varying manner in which articulate members of the nearly all white elite explained their racial hopes in terms of prevailing racial theories. When scientific racism penetrated Brazil at the end of the nineteenth century, intellectuals responded by trying to produce a rationale for their social system within the framework of scientific-racist thought. Even when those theories fell into scientific disrepute in the 1920s, the Brazilian elite maintained its explicit faith in the whitening process. Since faith could no longer be couched in the language of racial superiority and inferiority, it was described as a process of "ethnic integration," which was (as had been said since the 1890s) miraculously resolving Brazil's racial problems. As the hope for whitening remained constant, confidence in its inevitability grew.

While still believing that white was best and that Brazil was getting whiter, elite spokesmen after 1930 gained further satisfaction and confidence from the new scientific consensus that black was not inherently worse and thus that the racist claim that miscegenation must result in degeneration was nonsense. For approximately two decades after 1930, this Brazilian satisfaction at the discrediting of scientific-racism led to the argument that Brazilians' alleged lack of discrimination made them morally superior to the technologically more advanced countries, where systematic repression of racial minorities was still practiced. The United States was the favorite example; Nazi Germany became another. Comparisons with the United States had long been frequent in Brazilian writing about race, but they seemed even more striking after 1930, when the Jim Crow system had lost the intellectual sanction once given it by racist theory. Brazilians, who had always found themselves on the defensive in discussing their country's racial past and future, began to take the offensive. It was not the facts of Brazilian race relations that had changed, but the assumptions on which Brazilians argued.

What have Brazilians said about their ethnic identity since the early 1950s? On the one hand, there has been a tendency to believe that no problem exists. For the 1970 national census, for example, no data were collected according to race. A principal reason given for the decision was that previous data had been notoriously unreliable, since definitions of racial category (and even more, their application in individual cases) lacked uniformity.[63] However true it may be, the result was that researchers (and therefore the public and politicians) were deprived of nationwide figures on how nonwhites have fared in health, education, income, and jobs. In effect, the military-controlled government (1964–1985) declared that race was not a meaningful category in Brazil, at least for statistical purposes. This attitude has been paralleled by the relative lack of public discussion (aided by military government censorship) of race relations.

By the 1980 census, the technocrats and social science researchers had prevailed and race was again included. For the first time, Brazilians had a range of nationally collected data never before available. It showed without a doubt that the darker the skin the lower the standard of living. These data have only slowly begun to intrude into the elite political consciousness. Brazilians of color have also been slow to use the data to press for changes in social policy. A small black power movement, centered primarily in Rio de Janeiro and São Paulo, began in the late 1970s to challenge aggressively the prevalent myth of racial democracy. The centenary of abolition in 1988 offered an ideal occasion for debates over race relations, but the rhetoric seemed as unlikely as ever to affect social policy.[64]

Even these discussions are often terminated by the charge from other Brazilians that any attempt to heighten racial self-consciousness would be "racist."[65] In effect, Brazilian opinion makers are still living with the intellectual legacy of the compromise their parents and grandparents struck with racist theory. They are still implicit believers in a whiter Brazil, even though it may no longer be respectable to say so. They have inherited a richly complex multiracial society but have not yet found a new rationale to describe or justify its future.

Notes

This chapter draws extensively on two earlier works by the author: "Brazilian Intellectuals and the Problem of Race, 1870–1930," *Occasional Paper No. 6 of the Graduate Center for Latin American Studies, Vanderbilt University* (1969) and *Black into White: Race and Nationality in Brazilian Thought* (New York: Oxford University Press, 1974).

1. Carl N. Degler, *Neither Black nor White* (New York: Macmillan, 1971). For an analogous approach, see Thomas E. Skidmore, "Toward a Comparative Analysis of Race Relations since Abolition in Brazil and the United States," *Journal of Latin American Studies* 4, pt. 1 (May 1972): 1–28. For a survey of recent historiography on slavery (with references to abolition and post-abolition race relations), see Stuart B. Schwartz, "Recent Trends in the Study of Slavery in Brazil," *Luso-Brazilian Review* 25, no. 1 (Summer 1988): 1–25. There is an obvious difficulty in finding appropriate terms in English to discuss racial categories as used in Brazil in these years. *Negro* was probably the most frequent term for nonwhites. To designate that

category I have used "Afro-Brazilian." *Preto* normally meant very dark and is here translated as "black." *Mulatto* referred to an intermediate physical type, which could vary from relatively light skinned to relatively dark skinned. For that category I have used the identical word in English. Not included in this chapter is any systematic discussion of the Brazilian intellectual and political elite's attitudes toward the indigenous population.

2. Brazilian race relations have recently come in for increasing scholarly attention. For an overview as of the early 1980s, see Pierre-Michel Fontaine, ed., *Race, Class and Power in Brazil* (Los Angeles: Center for Afro-American Studies, UCLA, 1985). My chapter in that volume suggests some reasons for the recent interest. For a brief survey, which includes a highly useful annotated bibliography, see Carlos A. Hasenbalg, *Race Relations in Modern Brazil* (Albuquerque: Latin American Institute, University of New Mexico, n.d.), which is in "The Brazilian Curriculum Guide Specialized Bibliography," edited by Sam Adamo and Jon M. Tolman. Hasenbalg has also written one of the most comprehensive analyses of the evolution of Brazilian race relations in *Descriminação e desigualdades raciais no Brasil* (Rio de Janeiro: Graal, 1979). For an example of recent research on race relations in the post-abolition era, see George Reid Andrews, "Black Workers and White: São Paulo, Brazil, 1888–1928," *Hispanic American Historical Review* 50, 3 (August 1988): 491–524. My concentration in this chapter on elite thought can be partially justified on the grounds that in these years it was largely the elite that made and administered social policy. It is also true that elite thought and rule powerfully influenced nonelite behavior, as all classes were socialized into the acceptance of such ideas as whitening. Nonetheless, nonelite thought and behavior urgently need study.

3. An excellent analysis of this liberal ideology is to be found in Roque Spencer Maciel de Barros, *A ilustração brasileira e a idéia de universidade* (São Paulo: Universidade de São Paulo, 1959). See also Richard Graham, *Britain and the Onset of Modernization in Brazil, 1850–1914* (Cambridge: Cambridge University Press, 1968), chap. 10. The most penetrating overview of Brazilian liberalism as it evolved in the nineteenth century is Emília Viotti da Costa, *The Brazilian Empire: Myths and Histories* (Chicago: University of Chicago Press, 1985), chap. 3.

4. Gilberto Freyre, *Casa grande e senzala* (Rio de Janeiro: José Olympio, 1933); idem, *Sobrados e mocambos* (São Paulo: José Olympio, 1936); Frank Tannenbaum, *Slave and Citizen: The Negro in the Americas* (New York: Knopf, 1946).

5. Marvin Harris, *Patterns of Race in the Americas* (New York: Walker, 1964). There is a very useful analysis of the differing interpretations of Brazilian slavery in Viotti da Costa, *The Brazilian Empire*, chap. 9.

6. Instituto Brasileiro de Geografia e Estatística, *O Brasil em números* (Rio de Janeiro: IBGE, 1966), p. 25.

7. The most famous abolitionist document was Joaquim Nabuco's *O abolicionismo* (London: Abraham Kingdon, 1883), which has been published in English as *Abolitionism: The Brazilian Antislavery Struggle*, translated and edited by Robert

Conrad (Urbana: University of Illinois Press, 1977). The Abolitionist Society's manifesto, written largely by Nabuco and published in Rio in 1880 is reprinted in Osvaldo Melo Braga, ed., *Bibliografia de Joaquim Nabuco,* Instituto Nacional do Livro, Coleção Bl. Bibliografia, 8 (Rio de Janeiro: Imprensa Nacional, 1952): 14–23. The process of abolition has been well studied in Robert Brent Toplin, *The Abolition of Slavery in Brazil* (New York: Atheneum, 1972) and Robert Conrad, *The Destruction of Brazilian Slavery, 1850–1888* (Berkeley: University of California Press, 1972).

8. Antonio Gomes de Azevedo Sampaio, *Abolicionismo: considerações gerais do movimento anti-escravista e sua história limitada a Jacarehy, que foi um centro de acção no norte do estado de São Paulo* (São Paulo: n.p., 1890), pp. 12–13; [A. Coelho Rodrigues], *Manual do subdito fiel ou cartas de um lavrador a Sua Majestade o Imperador sobre a questão do elemento servil* (Rio de Janeiro: Moreira Maximo, 1884), pp. 6–7.

9. André Pinto Rebouças, *Agricultura nacional: estudos econômicos* (Rio de Janeiro: Lamoureux, 1883).

10. Nabuco, *Abolicionismo*, p. 223.

11. José do Patrocínio, editorial in *Gazeta da Tarde* for May 5, 1887, reprinted in Afonso Celso, *Oito anos de Parlamento, poder pessoal de D. Pedro II* (São Paulo: Melhoramentos, 1928?), pp. 131–132. Joaquim Nabuco was scandalized that José Veríssimo should have described Machado de Assis as a "mulatto" in his obituary of the great novelist. Nabuco wrote Veríssimo in 1908 that "for me Machado was a white man, and I believe that he became one. If there was any strange blood it did not at all affect his perfectly Caucasian character" (Osvaldo Melo Braga, ed., *Bibliografia de Joaquim Nabuco,* p. 170). For a study that focuses on race as a central theme in nineteenth-century and early twentieth-century Brazilian literature, see David T. Haberly, *Three Sad Races: Racial Identity and National Consciousness in Brazilian Literature* (Cambridge: Cambridge University Press, 1983).

12. Henry Koster, *Travels in Brazil* (London: Longman, 1816), p. 391.

13. Joaquim Nabuco, *Obras completas*, v. 11: *Discursos parlamentares 1879–1889* (São Paulo: Instituto Progresso, 1949), pp. 59–67; Barros, *A ilustração brasileira,* pp. 102–103. Vigorous opposition to the coolie proposal, also based on an explicit desire to get "new blood," not "old juice" from "degenerate bodies," was expressed by João Cardoso Menezes e Sousa [Barão de Paranapiacaba], *Teses sobre colonização do Brasil: projeto de solução as questões sociais que se prendem a este difícil problema* (Rio de Janeiro: Typ. Nacional, 1875), pp. 418–423.

14. Gilberto Freyre, *Ordem e progresso* (Rio de Janeiro: José Olympio, 1959), I: clx–clxi.

15. (Chicago: University of Chicago Press, 1944; first edition 1902 of *Os Sertões*). Raimundo Nina Rodrigues, *Os Africanos no Brasil,* 3d ed. (São Paulo: Ed. Nacional, 1945), esp. the introduction and chap. 8. Gilberto Freyre talked frankly of Rodrigues' racist ideas in his introduction to Augusto Lins e Silva, *Atualidade*

de Nina Rodrigues (Rio de Janeiro: Leitura, 1945). A useful bibliography of Rodrigues' widely scattered works is included in Henrique L. Alves, *Nina Rodrigues e o negro do Brasil* (São Paulo: Asociação Cultural do Negro, [1962?]). Cesare Lombroso, the Italian physician and criminologist, argued that criminals were an atavistic throwback to an earlier stage of evolution.

16. Euclides da Cunha, *Os sertões*, 2d ed. (Rio de Janeiro: Laemmert, 1903), pp. 108–113; Gilberto Freyre, *Atualidade de Euclides da Cunha* (Rio de Janeiro: Casa do Estudante do Brasil, 1943); Clovis Moura, *Introdução ao pensamento de Euclides da Cunha* (Rio de Janeiro: Civilização Brasileira, 1964), chap. 5. In a letter in 1903 Euclides explained, "I am a disciple of Gumplowicz" (Francisco Venâncio Filho, *Euclides da Cunha e seus amigos* [São Paulo: Ed. Nacional, 1938], p. 86).

17. James Bryce, *South America: Observations and Impressions* (New York: Macmillan, 1912), pp. 401–420.

18. Otto Prazeres, "Aspectos do Rio Branco," *Revista do Instituto Histórico e Geográfico Brasileiro,* 244 (July–September 1959): 343–345; Freyre, *Ordem e progresso,* I: xlix, cl–cli. Euclides' relationship with the foreign minister is documented in Francisco Venâncio Filho, *Rio Branco e Euclides da Cunha* (Rio de Janeiro: Ministerio das Relações Exteriores, 1946).

19. José Veríssimo, review in *Jornal do Commercio* (Rio de Janeiro), December 4, 1889.

20. A useful introduction to these opponents of racist thought may be found in Guerreiro Ramos, *Introdução crítica à sociologia brasileira* (Rio de Janeiro: Andes, 1957).

21. Alberto Torres, *O problema nacional brasileiro* (Rio de Janeiro: Imprensa Nacional, 1914), p. 49; idem, *Le problème mondial* (Rio de Janeiro: Imprensa Nacional, 1913), p. 138.

22. Torres, *O problema nacional brasileiro*, p. 9; idem, *Le problème mondial*, p. 141.

23. For a more detailed analysis of the wartime period, see Thomas E. Skidmore, *Black into White: Race and Nationality in Brazilian Thought* (New York: Oxford University Press, 1974), chap. 5. The Brazilian case is placed within a wider context in Bill Albert, *South America and the First World War* (Cambridge: Cambridge University Press, 1988). One can gain the full flavor of turn-of-the-century elite Rio culture in Jeffrey Needell, *A Tropical Belle Epoque* (Cambridge: Cambridge University Press, 1987).

24. Torres, *Le problème mondial*, pp. xvi, 179; idem, *As fontes da vida no Brasil* (Rio de Janeiro: Imprensa Nacional, 1915), pp. 7–8, 39.

25. Alvaro Bomilcar, *O preconceito de raça no Brasil* (Rio de Janeiro: Aurora, 1916). Although written in 1911, the book was withheld from publication for five years, according to the author, in hopes of a more receptive atmosphere.

26. The manifesto of the Propaganda Nativista group is reprinted in Alvaro Bomilcar, *A política no Brasil ou o nacionalismo radical* (Rio de Janeiro: Leite Ribeiro, 1920), pp. 179–181.

27. José Maria Belo, *Ensaios políticos e literários: Ruy Barbosa e escritos diversos* (Rio de Janeiro: Castilho, 1918), p. 177.

28. An influential collection of articles by members of this generation may be found in A. Carneiro Leão et al., *À margem da história da República* (Rio de Janeiro: Annuario do Brasil, 1924). In the unsigned preface the contributors are said to "read and admire" Alberto Torres, whose work "has not been read carefully by the generation that preceded us." For a more detailed treatment of Sílvio Romero, a key thinker of his generation, see Skidmore, *Black into White*, pp. 32–37.

29. F. J. Oliveira Vianna, *Populações meridionais do Brasil*, 2 vols., 5th ed. (São Paulo: José Olympio, 1952), I: 13.

30. F. J. Oliveira Vianna, "O povo brasileiro e sua evolução," in Ministério da Agricultura, Indústria e Commercio, Directoria Geral de Estatística, *Recenseamento do Brasil realizado em 1 de Setembro de 1920*, vol. 1: *Introducção* (Rio de Janeiro, 1922), pp. 279–400. It was later published separately as *Evolução do povo brasileiro* (Rio de Janeiro, 1956).

31. Vianna, *Evolução do povo brasileiro*, pp. 178–182, 188–190.

32. The official explanation for the dropping of race was given in "Histórico e instrucções para a execução do recenseamento de 1920," *Recenseamento do Brazil realizado em 1 de Setembro 1920*, I: 488–489.

33. Very favorable reviews of the first volume of *Populações meridionais do Brasil* came from influential younger literary critics, who were generally identified with the reaction against the intellectual assumptions of the older generation. Alceu Amoroso Lima, for example, praised the book on December 27, 1920, hardly mentioning Vianna's Aryanism: Lima, *Estudos literários*, 2 vols. (Rio de Janeiro: Aguilar, 1966), I: 292–296.

34. For a brief survey of studies of the African and Afro-Brazilian, see as a starting point Artur Ramos, *O negro na civilização brasileira* (Rio de Janeiro: Casa do Estudante do Brasil, 1956), chap. 14; and José Honório Rodrigues, *Brazil and Africa* (Berkeley: University of California Press, 1965), pp. 36–52.

35. Sílvio Romero, *História da literatura brasileira*, 2 vols. (Rio de Janeiro: Garnier, 1888). The most inclusive work by Raimundo Nina Rodrigues was *Os africanos no Brasil* (São Paulo: Ed. Nacional, 1932), a posthumous edition of papers edited by Homero Pires.

36. João do Rio [João Paulo Coelho Barreto], *As religiões no Rio* (Rio de Janeiro: Garnier, 1906). A collection of papers was published in Manoel Querino, *Costumes africanos no Brasil* (Rio de Janeiro: Civilização Brasileira, 1938). See also Querino, *The African Contribution to Brazilian Civilization*, translated by E. Bradford Burns (Tempe: Center for Latin American Studies, Arizona State University, 1978). Information on this relatively little-known writer may be found in Gonçalo de Athayde Pereira, *Prof. Manuel Querino: sua vida e suas obras* (Bahia: Imprensa Oficial do Estado, 1932).

37. Alvaro Lins, *Ensaio sobre Roquette-Pinto e a ciência como literatura* (Rio de Janeiro: Ed. de Ouro, 1967); Pedro Gouvea Filho, *E. Roquette-Pinto: o antropólogo*

e educador (Rio de Janeiro: Ministério da Educação e Cultura, Instituto Nacional de Cinema Educativo, 1955). The shift in scientific thought about race among anthropologists is traced in George Stocking, *Race, Culture and Evolution* (London: Collier-Macmillan, 1968); detail on American thinking may be found also in I. A. Newby, *Jim Crow's Defense: Anti-Negro Thought in America, 1900–1930* (Baton Rouge: Louisiana State University Press, 1965).

38. The quotations are taken from "O Brasil e a antropogeografia," reprinted in Edgar Roquette-Pinto, *Seixos rolados* (Rio de Janeiro: Mendonça Machado, 1927), pp. 45–79, which is identified there as a lecture delivered in 1912, although one biographer (Gouvea Filho, *Roquette-Pinto*, p. 14) dates it as September 1914.

39. Among Ramos' many publications are *As culturas negras no mundo novo* (Rio de Janeiro: Civilização Brasileira, 1937), and *O folk-lore negro do Brasil* (Rio de Janeiro: Civilização Brasileira, 1935).

40. Gilberto Freyre, *The Masters and the Slaves*, translated by Samuel Putnam (2d ed. New York: Knopf, 1956). The first American edition was published in 1946. The first Brazilian edition of *Casa grande e senzala* was published in Rio de Janeiro in 1933 by José Olympio.

41. *Sobrados e mucambos* was first published in São Paulo in 1936 by José Olympio. An extensively revised second edition was published in 1951, and a third edition appeared in 1961. The first edition was subtitled "Decadência do Patriarchado Rural no Brasil," to which was added in the subtitle of the second edition "e desenvolvimento do urbano." The American edition, *The Mansions and the Shanties*, was translated and edited by Harriet de Onís (New York: Knopf, 1963).

42. Freyre has explained how he had to be liberated from an ethnic inferiority complex about Brazil. Describing his graduate studies in anthropology at Columbia University in the early 1920s, Freyre wrote, "Once upon a time, after three straight years of absence from my country, I caught sight of a group of Brazilian seamen— mulattoes and *cafusos* [mixture of Indian and black]—crossing Brooklyn Bridge. I no longer remember whether they were from [the] *São Paulo* or from [the] *Minas Gerais* [referring to the names of Brazilian ships in harbor], but I know that they impressed me as being the caricatures of men, and there came to mind a phrase from a book on Brazil written by an American traveler: 'the fearfully mongrel aspect of the population.' That was the sort of thing to which miscegenation led. I ought to have had someone to tell me what Roquette Pinto had told the Aryanizers of the Brazilian Eugenics Congress in 1929: that these individuals whom I looked upon as representative of Brazil were not simply *mulattoes* or *cafusos* but sickly ones. It was my studies in anthropology under the direction of Professor Boas that first revealed to me the Negro and the mulatto for what they are—with the effects of enviroment or cultural experience separated from racial characteristics" (*The Masters and the Slaves*, pp. xxvi–xxvii).

43. João Cruz Costa, *Contribuição à história das idéias no Brasil* (Rio de Janeiro: José Olympio, 1956), p. 440. The extraordinary influence of *Casa grande e senzala* would have been impossible if Freyre had not been able to cite this scientific

evidence. His book therefore had to be based in part on the writings of other Brazilian investigators who had anticipated many of his questions. His accomplishment was to have transformed this evidence into a new approach to Brazilian history.

44. Freyre also provoked some intemperate dissent in Brazil. In 1939 the right-wing Catholic press labeled him "the Pornographer of Recife." See Samuel Putnam's article "Brazilian Literature," in the *Handbook of Latin American Studies* (1939), V: 357.

45. Freyre went on to develop his interpretation of Brazil's multiracial heritage in more controversial form. The third volume in his history of patriarchical society in Brazil (published in Brazil in 1959) covered the years between the founding of the Republic in 1889 and the end of World War I and analyzed the agony of the Brazilian elite as it faced up to the reality of a society that did not fit the soon-to-be archaic categories of scientific-racist thought: Freyre, *Ordem e progresso*. For a critical review, see Thomas E. Skidmore, "Gilberto Freyre and the Early Brazilian Republic: Some Notes on Methodology," *Comparative Studies in Society and History* 6, no. 4 (July 1964): 490–505. Even before World War II, Freyre had developed his theory of "Luso-tropicalism," which assumed a unique Portuguese gift for achieving supposedly harmonious multiracial societies, as in Freyre, *O mundo que o Português criou* (Rio de Janeiro: José Olympio, 1940).

46. Mário de Andrade, "O samba rural Paulista," *Revista do Arquivo Municipal* 41 (November 1937): 37–116; his chapter in Edgar Roquette-Pinto, ed., *Estudos afro-brasileiros* (Rio de Janeiro: Ed. Ariel, 1935).

47. Edison Carneiro, *Religiões negras* (Rio de Janeiro: Civilização Brasileira, 1936).

48. Fernando de Azevedo, *Brazilian Culture: An Introduction to the Study of Culture in Brazil*, translated by William Rex Crawford (New York, 1950), pp. 40–41. The first Brazilian edition was issued as an official government publication: Instituto Brasileiro de Geografia e Estatística, Commissão Censitária Nacional, *Recenseamento geral do Brasil*: National Series, vol. I: Introdução, vol. I: Fernando de Azevedo, *A cultura brasileira* (Rio de Janeiro, 1943).

49. Neiva cited Batista de Lacerda, Director of the National Museum, as the authority for his prediction of a century, after which "the entire world will consider us white, except for the United States which . . . today still considers the Portuguese people less than perfectly white because of the transfusion of Moorish blood." Neiva's article appeared in 1921 and is reprinted in Arthur Neiva, *Daqui e de longe: chrônicas nacionais e de viagem* (São Paulo: Melhoramentos, [1927?]), pp. 111–118.

50. The debate may be found in *Anais da Câmara dos Deputados*, 1921 (Rio de Janeiro, 1923), VI: 623–637. The debate was held on July 29, 1921.

51. Ibid., 1923 (Rio de Janeiro, 1928), X: 140–149. The debate took place on October 22, 1923.

52. E. Roquette-Pinto, *Ensaios de antropologia brasileira* (São Paulo: n.p.,

1933), pp. 69–75; Azevedo Amaral, *O comentário,* July 4, 1929; and *1°Congresso Brasileiro de Eugenia* (Rio de Janeiro: n.p., 1929). For an analysis of the Brazilian eugenics movement in the context of contemporary biological thought, see Nancy Leys Stepan, "Eugenics in Brazil, 1917–1940" in Mark Adams, ed.,*New Directions in the History of Eugenics* (forthcoming). The author concludes that the extreme eugenists (i.e., those wishing to engineer racial purity) gained no significant following in Brazil.

53. This story is told in Teresa Meade and Gregory Alonso Pirio, "In Search of the Afro-American 'Eldorado': Attempts by North American Blacks to Enter Brazil in the 1920s," *Luso-Brazilian Review* XXV, no. 1 (summer 1988): 85–110.

54. Fernando H. Mendes de Almeida, *Constituições do Brasil* (São Paulo: Saraiva, 1963), pp. 310–312.

55. The debate is reprinted in a collection of the speeches involving the São Paulo delegation: *Ação da bancada paulista "Por São Paulo unido" na Assemblea Constituinte* (São Paulo, 1935), pp. 364–413.

56. The constitutional provisions are in Mendes de Almeida, *Constituições*, pp. 470,664. For a discussion of the background of this legislation, see Manuel Diegues Júnior,*Imigração, urbanização e industrialização* (Rio de Janeiro: Centro Brasileiro de Pesquisas Educacionais, 1961), pp. 169–267.

57. For a study that puts the Integralist movement into the context of the radicalization of politics in the 1930s, see Robert M. Levine, *The Vargas Regime: The Critical Years, 1934–1938* (New York: Columbia University Press, 1970).

58. As, for example, in Gustavo Barroso, *O que o integralista deve saber* (Rio de Janeiro: Civilização Brasileira, 1935), pp. 119–133.

59. There is a succinct discussion of these measures in Karl Loewenstein, *Brazil under Vargas* (New York: Macmillan, 1942), pp. 205–211.

60. Detail on Nazi designs on southern Brazil may be found in Jurgen Hell, "Das 'sudbrasilianische Neudeutschland': Der annexionistische Grundzug der wilhelminischen und nazistischen Brasilienpolitik, 1895–1943," in*Der Deutsche Faschismus in Lateinamerika, 1933–1943* (Berlin, 1966), pp. 103–124.

61. Reprinted in Guerreiro Ramos, *Guerra e relações de raça* (Rio de Janeiro: União Brasileira de Estudantes, 1943), pp. 177–180.

62. Maria Luiza Tucci Carneiro, *O anti-semitismo na era Vargas* (São Paulo: Brasiliense 1988). See also the feature article on Aranha's policy in *Veja* (March 23, 1988), and the subsequent exchange of letters in *Veja* (April 13 and 27, 1988).

63. This issue was fully debated in a public session of the Comissão Censitária Nacional on September 9, 1969, where several leading sociologists presented their views. The commission decided by a split vote to exclude both race and religion from the 1970 census questionnaire: Instituto Brasileiro de Geografia e Estatística, Comissão Censitária Nacional, "Ata dos trabalhos: 6ª sessão ordinária, Setembro 9, 1969" (typescript).

64. An example of the better journalistic coverage is the photo-essay "Centenário de um mau século," *Veja* (May 11, 1988).

65. Edison Carneiro, for example, back in 1950 accused the organizers of the First Congress of the Brazilian Negro of trying to "enunciate racist statements" (Carneiro, *Ladinos e crioulos* [Rio de Janeiro: Civilização Brasileira, 1964], p. 116). The publication of the Brazilian edition of my *Black into White* (*Preto no Branco* [Rio de Janeiro: Ed. Paz e Terra, 1976]) led a columnist for the leading Rio daily to denounce American professors who try to introduce "an irrelevant discussion of the racial problem" (João Luiz Faria Netto, "Importação supérflua," *Jornal do Brasil,* July 17, 1976).

3. Race in Argentina and Cuba, 1880–1930: Theory, Policies, and Popular Reaction

ALINE HELG

At the end of the nineteenth century most of Hispanic America entered a period of economic growth. Exports, massive public works, railroads, electrification of some sections of the capitals, and new factories were all changes that gave the elite the impression that it was on the way to "modernization." But modernization was limited to a minority, mainly, the elite of major cities. For the bulk of the population, modernization meant little but an increase in the cost of living, the loss of land, proletarianization, and exploitation.

In social and demographic terms, the end of the nineteenth century and the early twentieth century were decades of considerable movement. This was apparent not only in the migration of newcomers (Europeans, Chinese, Japanese, and Lebanese), but also in the internal migration of landless peasants, Indians from dismembered communities, and emancipated slaves. Thus the contrast was sharp between the city centers and the outlying regions, between an educated elite living according to European standards and an illiterate poor population whose conditions had not visibly improved since independence. This contrast was also an ethnic one, for in many countries the elite was Creole (that is here, white of Spanish origin born in Hispanic America) and the popular classes Indian, black, mestizo, or mulatto.

In addition, since the end of the eighteenth century, the Hispanic American elite had been culturally dependent on France, England, the United States, and Germany. The French and American Revolutions had served as an inspiration to Creole liberators. In many respects, Hispanic American independence had been an illusion leading to new foreign ties for the elite and to the exclusion of the popular majority from the project of nation building. The elites visited Europe and the United States in search of models, while generally ignoring their own countries beyond the capitals. As a result, they identified more closely with Europeans than with their fellow countrymen. It is, therefore, no surprise to find this elite affected by European ideas regarding race.

Between 1880 and 1930, Hispanic American intellectuals were strongly influenced by positivism, social Darwinism, geographical determinism, and many racial theories emanating from Europe.[1] Racism—as a "rationalized pseudo-scientific theory positing the innate and permanent inferiority of nonwhites"—accompanied

European colonialism and U.S. imperialism.[2] To elite Hispanic Americans tending to view their own reality in relation to European and North American models, the racist explanation of human diversity proved attractive. The racial issue pervaded numerous essays in Hispanic America that discussed the Indian "problem," the black "question," the consequences of "cross-breeding," or the possible emergence of a new Latin American race. Moreover, for a substantial portion of the elite, the rapid urbanization that brought darker people to the cities, as well as the emergence of the mestizos and mulattoes in politics represented a threat to their power monopoly and were interpreted as manifestations of race struggle. Civil wars and the failure of postindependence democratic institutions were attributed to the racial inferiority of Latin America. This justified the dominance of a Creole elite—at least until the masses had the potential to live in a democracy. In addition, comparison with the United States induced Hispanic Americans to single out race as the main difference. The United States had developed because it was a nation of Anglo-Saxon immigrants in which the Indians had been pushed aside and the blacks segregated. As a consequence, European immigration appeared to be the key for Hispanic American civilization and modernization.

Racial theories, with their local flavor, were embraced by the Hispanic American elite until approximately the 1920s, despite some exceptions. For some forty years, although they were never rigorously implemented, these theories influenced contemporary policy making, particularly regarding immigration, education, and Indian affairs. In the 1920s, although they did not totally disappear, they were silenced by various other movements, such as *indigenismo,* socialism, *hispanidad,* and nationalism, that gradually replaced the terminology of race with that of class or social group.

I have chosen to illustrate the Hispanic American racial issue by reference to two countries: Argentina and Cuba. By 1900 Argentina had almost completed one century of independence. It had fulfilled the dream of its elite, as expressed in 1852 by Juan Bautista Alberdi's *Bases:*[3] it had become a nation of predominantly European stock. This had been possible through massive immigration, wars of extermination against the Indians, and the drowning of the blacks in the immigrant waves. Its economy had developed rapidly through agricultural production, and industrialization was in sight. Simultaneously, various Argentinean intellectuals theorized about their country's change and partly linked it to racial evolution. Influential on the intelligentsia of other Latin American nations, they tended to impose Argentina as the example to follow, as well as contributing decidedly to the diffusion of European racial theories in the area.

Cuba only achieved independence from Spain in 1898, thanks to the heavy participation in the liberation wars of Afro-Cubans on the side of Creoles. (Blacks and mulattoes took an active part in the island's economy and society. In addition, Afro-Cuban intellectuals played a fundamental role in forging Cuban identity against Spain throughout the nineteenth century.) Thus, almost a century after Argentina's independence, Cuba faced the problem of building a nation with a very different ethnic balance. No project of racial integration, however, emerged from the Creole leading class. It stuck to the old hope of Cuban politician and prominent abolitionist José Antonio Saco (1797–1879), that the blacks would disappear once the slave trade ended because of massive white immigration and miscegenation.[4] Many Creole intellectuals proposed to imitate Argentina's process of "whitening" through European immigration in order to achieve economic development and civilization.

Thus, I shall explore—first with regard to Argentina and then to Cuba—the racial thinking of a few leading intellectuals who played a dominant part in that issue, but who are now either neglected or studied in relation to other subjects. Then I shall briefly examine the relationship between race theorizing and national reality. I shall also explore the links relating the issue of race to government policies, especially on immigration, education, and crime, as well as to movements of popular protest.

Race Theorizing in Argentina: The Glorification of "Whitening"

Argentina's rapid ethnic change, coupled with its economic expansion, led most intellectuals to glorify the Europeanization of their country: it had vast space, fertile land, and a mainly white population; no doubt it was to play a leading role in the world of tomorrow.[5] They based their interpretation of Latin America and Argentina on the work of social Darwinist and positivist Europeans or on North American writings about race, psychology, and history.[6]

I shall give special attention to three intellectuals who were broadly read in Argentina and throughout Latin America, where they served as models for other essayists: statesman and educator Domingo Faustino Sarmiento (1811–1888), who in the 1880s, pointed to race as accounting for a multitude of Latin American problems; lawyer and educationalist Carlos Octavio Bunge (1875–1918), who wrote *Nuestra América* in 1903, a book almost forgotten today but famous at the time; and physician and sociologist José Ingenieros (1877–1925), who is little studied for his racial theorizing. They were among the few to present a global analysis of their racial reality that transcended the mere reproduction of European theories.

In the 1880s Sarmiento was torn between an evolutionary vision of race and a faith in immigration and education as the solution to Argentina's modernization problems. If the races had had a remote common origin, he wrote, a worldwide cataclysm had divided the continents; as a result, people evolving in distinct environments had progressively formed different races. Moreover, distinct races had developed at different rates, the slowest being the Indians and the blacks, the fastest, the whites. In Sarmiento's judgment, there was no doubt that the Anglo-Saxon and Christian United States was the very incarnation of the most civilized race. But the so-called inferior races were not excluded from future evolution through education, "because," he argued, "the progress of intelligence is sure and unfailing in all of them, even the most backward."[7]

He tended, however, to be more confident about the ability of blacks to progress than of the Indians. The latter appeared to him as a "prehistoric race," a sort of living testimony of our ancestors. He denounced their widespread and, he said, congenital, alcoholism, laziness, and ignorance of such "civilized virtues" as private property, use of money, free enterprise, and democracy. As for Argentina's Indians, he considered the eastern Guaranís and the southern Araucanians as nothing more than stubborn animals with no capacity for civilization.⁸ In the mid-1860s, as a plenipotentiary minister in the United States, Sarmiento eagerly opposed the American press' sympathy for the Guaranís in the Paraguayan War, defending his country's action. As a president of Argentina (1868–1874), he ordered several military expeditions against the "barbarous" Indians.

On the other hand, for Sarmiento the Africans were childish and "races that God [was] reserving for future worlds, maybe for the one being prepared by Livingstone, Stanley, and Brazza."⁹ He described the Afro-Americans as the most demonstrative race, enthusiastic, faithful, and, of course, fond of dance; but their vanishing in Argentina provoked no regret in him.

In viewing the Europeans, Sarmiento had little regard for the Spaniards, whose brains had supposedly been atrophied by five centuries of Inquisition, a damage aggravated among Spanish Americans by their intermarriage with races with an even lesser brain. As a result, people of Spanish descent lacked the faculties for self-government and democracy that, he thought, belonged to the superior Anglo-Saxons. This is why Sarmiento hoped that, together with appropriate education, Anglo-Saxon immigration could transform the mentality of Argentina. He deplored the fact that his country had attracted, instead, a majority of Latins. In addition, he accepted the theory that by intermarrying with inferior races whites were not transmitting their worthy qualities. Although he was not absolutely pessimistic about Argentina's particular future, in the never-completed conclusions of his *Conflicto y armonía* he contradicted the dominant racial thought of the 1880s about the inevitable triumph of the whites in the worldwide struggle. He expressed a nonevolutionary fear that Latin American whites would eventually be absorbed into the vanquished races if they did not overcome their egoism and give comprehensive primary education to the indigenous masses.¹⁰

In *Nuestra América* Carlos Octavio Bunge aimed at a global analysis of Latin America focusing on what he considered to be its key problem: its ethnic composition. In 317 pages padded with contradictions, personal justifications, and many nonracist allegations,¹¹ he pretended to build a theory of concordance between physical (or racial) and psychological characteristics, much in the vein of the French theorist Gustave Le Bon.¹² Once again, Anglo-Saxons appeared at the top of the racial scale, with great sentiment and altruism as their major traits, as well as industry, joy, and democracy.¹³ Spaniards, in contrast, suffered from having a peninsular geography that had attracted invasions and from subsequent intermarriage with Arabs, Jews, Berbers, and Africans, through which they became Afro-Europeans. As a result, Spaniards developed arrogance, a psychological characteristic explaining at one and the same time the Inquisition, their emphasis on *limpieza de sangre*, and prodigality, ostentation, fatalism, economic misery, and laziness.[14]

Bunge, like Sarmiento, believed in the superiority of blacks over Indians in the struggle for life. He acknowledged their stamina for hard work and their alleged fecundity, the sense of joy and democracy he believed they had brought to Spanish America. However, "until now in no climate and under no government did [the blacks] render leading intellectual service to humanity." And Bunge ascribed two fundamental characteristics to all blacks: "servility and infatuation, reciprocally complementary."[15]

As for the Indians, their long isolation had made them almost a distinct species. Nevertheless, their Asiatic origin classified them in the yellow race and gave them the common psychological trait of "Oriental fatalism," the key to the easy conquest of most Indians and their general sadness. However, Bunge needed a different trait to account for the long resistance of Argentinean and North American Indians: he singled out a supposed passion for revenge produced by an extreme sensibility to fear. This led him to the following formula: "The native American is either exaggeratedly fatalistic or exaggeratedly vengeful."[16] In any event, both types of Indians, belonging to an inferior race, were to disappear, either by slow absorption into the dominant culture or by extermination.[17]

Consequently, Bunge labeled intermarriage with Indians as "hybridism," while the same union between Africans and Spaniards benefited from their common origin. Following Le Bon, he believed that any "cross-breed" was characterized by a lack of psychological balance or moral sense, as a result of such dual ancestry. But then he conceived from Swiss naturalist Louis Agassiz' puzzling theory of hybrids' sterility a new theory of "selective degenerative sterility," ranging from "agenesis" (or total sterility of the hybrid) to "eugenesis" (or total fecundity of the hybrids). However, he could not ignore the fact that in Latin America eugenesis was the rule. Thus, he specified, in Latin America sterility was extremely relative and limited to very uncommon intermarriage involving altogether Indian, African, and Chinese parentage.[18] Bunge's stubborn attempt to mesh his reality with this by-then much controverted theory reveals the racist fundamentals of his interpretation.

Although *Nuestra América's* aim was to describe the illness of the continent, Bunge did not give much attention to possible remedies. In a hasty conclusion, he proposed education, cultural Europeanization, and hard work, all three contradicting, in fact, his deterministic theory relating race to psychology. Also contradicting his condemnation of miscegenation was his patriotic faith in the brilliant future of Argentina, with immigration progressively annihilating ethnic differences between the people of the interior and those of the littoral, and turning the shortcomings of the Creole into positive qualities: arrogance would become candor; laziness, work; and sadness, joy.[19] "There will be only one unique Argentinean type, as imaginative as the aborigine of the tropics and as practical as the dweller of the cold climates, one complex and complete type, which could appear to be the total man, the model of the modern man: Ecce homo!"[20] Although full of contradictions, Bunge's work was written with such forcefulness and style that it captured the imagination of the elite in other countries besides Argentina and had an intellectual influence far beyond the actual qualities of his argument.

With José Ingenieros, doubts and contradictions vanished. This self-designated socialist was a firm admirer of French theorists Ernest Renan and Count Arthur de Gobineau. He stood for coherent and intransigent racial evolutionism in Argentina and he believed in the theory of "biogenetical correlation" between environment, climate, race, institutions, and beliefs. A strong conviction about the merits of natural selection and racial inequality led him to affirm that "colored" races were inferior and not adaptable to "white" civilization. Thus their fate was to disappear in the evolutionary racial struggle and give way to the whites. This process, however, was slowed down in the areas of "inferior climate," such as intertropical America, where Europeans had difficulty in adapting.[21]

According to Ingenieros, Indians simply had no future, so he did not discuss their condition.[22] Blacks inspired his most racist writing. They supposedly suffered physical inferiority, while their mental power and feelings resembled those of domestic animals, so much that even Dutch naturalist Eugene Dubois' *Pithecanthropus* would be ashamed of them.[23] Everything, from their way of living to their illiteracy and lack of religiousness, alienated them from humanity. These allegations led to Ingenieros' justification of black slavery, "which would be the political and legal sanction of a purely biological reality."[24] He further advocated the complete denial of blacks' participation in democracy: "Men of colored races should not be politically and juridically our equal; they are unfit for the exercise of civil rights and they should not be juridically considered as 'individuals.'"[25] Thus everything undertaken in favor of the blacks would be unscientific: the best solution would be to protect them so that they could pleasantly pass away.[26]

However, Ingenieros did not accept inequality within the white race. In his view, the contemporaneous superiority of Anglo-Saxons over Latins was merely historical, political, and economic, not anthropological, and the alleged differences between dolicocephalics and brachycephalics, between Semites and Aryans, had not been scientifically proved. His essay entitled "Simulación en la lucha por la vida en el orden biológico y social" (1903) showed well his differential treatment of the white race as compared to the "inferior" races. He denied the possibility of racial war among civilized nations except through "simulation" (that is, using the myth of original races), because of the nonexistence of the so-called different European races; he also denounced French anti-Semitism in the Dreyfus affair as a mask for a clerico-military reactionary program. But when he took a worldwide perspective, he went back to the social Darwinist schema of racial struggles: "The inferior races massively disappear, being destroyed; their best elements manage to adapt to the superior races. Out of the latter only the most selected groups survive, slowly but inevitably intermarrying among themselves, not leaving one single civilized people able to claim the title of ethnic purity."[27]

In other words, as races, the darker would vanish and only the white survive.

However, the latter would be a mixture of the various ethnic groups belonging to the white race, together with the fittest individuals of the darker races, who would have had the necessary qualities for integration into the superior race (and thus "whiten"). In the Americas English colonization had had racial consequences opposite to those of Spanish colonization. The English were pure Europeans who avoided mixing with the "colored" races, thus improving their biological stock. Spaniards were Arabo-Europeans, who intermarried with Indians and blacks, thus debilitating their race. So what should be done to redeem Latin America? Favor European immigration and education, and keep the nonwhites in subordinate positions in line with their supposedly limited abilities.[28]

Thus, Ingenieros was highly optimistic about the future of Argentina. Although colonial miscegenation had set back the formation of a white nation by at least a century, the waves of white immigration of the nineteenth and twentieth centuries had eventually brought to Argentina all the qualities that supposedly belonged to the superior race: work, culture, democracy, and modernization.[29] Even the political voting record was related by Ingenieros to racial, not socioeconomic, factors: "The electoral map of the republic coincides with the map of the races. The leftist democratic parties (Radical, Socialist, Liga del Sur, and similar groups) have their greatest influence in the most Europeanized regions of the country."[30] The lower races were vanishing and, through intermarriage, the characteristics of the superior races were coming to predominate, leading to the disappearance of the "half-breeds." The Argentineans were becoming "a new variety of the European white races."[31] Ingenieros went so far as to announce that Argentina would play "a tutelary function over the other republics of the continent" because of its racial superiority.[32]

From Racism to Xenophobia in Argentina

In reality, the whitening of Argentina through immigration had been a fast process. In 1869 Indians represented 5 percent of the population, but by 1895, only 0.7 percent of a total of 3,955,000. The blacks, centered in Buenos Aires, had composed 25 percent of the capital's population in 1838, but had dropped to 2 percent by 1887. Between 1880 and 1930, total net immigration added nearly 3,225,000 inhabitants to Argentina. Among the immigrants, 43 percent were Italian and 34 percent Spanish; far behind came the highly valued Anglo-Saxons. As for the Jews, during the peak years of 1907 to 1914, they represented between 2 and 6 percent of total net immigration.[33]

In this context, Sarmiento's, Bunge's, and Ingenieros' theorizing appeared closer to their European models than to the changing reality of Argentina. By the end of the nineteenth century, the themes of blacks, Indians, and miscegenation were losing their currency in favor of the debates regarding immigrants. Reduced to an invisible minority, blacks were further pushed aside by newcomers ready to start their upward mobility from lower urban positions. Afro-Argentineans remained in professions requiring Argentinean citizenship, such as the armed forces and lower-level civil service, or as washerwomen and musicians. But they no longer represented a threat to the Creole ruling class. They were discriminated against, but no specific policy was designed for this end. In fact, their "natural" vanishing puzzled more than one essayist. Sarmiento, in his desire to see a white America, attributed the process to the secret action of affinity and repulsion. Bunge imputed it to Buenos Aires' climate, to the inability of the blacks' lungs to resist the pampa's winds, to intermarrying with whites, and to the waves of European immigration; elsewhere he blessed alcoholism, smallpox, and tuberculosis for having decimated the capital's nonwhite population. Ingenieros added the devastating effects of the wars of independence and the civil wars of the nineteenth century.[34]

The Indians, however, were considered the most challenging enemy of Argentinean civilization until the early 1880s. In 1879, Gen. Julio A. Roca initiated his Conquest of the Desert, a misnamed war that expanded the Argentinean frontier westward and southward by subduing or exterminating entire aboriginal groups. Heavy military mobilization against the Indians continued well into the 1880s. By 1890, most of Argentina's Indians had been either killed or enslaved, that is, forcibly incorporated into the army, taken by soldiers as concubines, assigned to sugar mills as peons or to Buenos Aires' families as servants. A few were confined to reservations, and some managed to escape. It was not until the 1930s, however, that sporadic military attacks against the few surviving Indians came to an end. Alternative policies were hardly discussed.[35]

The question of how to civilize and train the subdued Indians was repeatedly raised by the executive power and the Congress. Although a few advocated the protection of Indian communities in subsidized reservations, for most politicians the best and cheapest solution was to disperse the "savages" and roughly rehabilitate them through military service, agricultural labor, or domestic service.[36] No health policy was promoted for them after such deportation, and many died from diseases they were not immunized against. In a country where much importance was conferred on public education, no instruction was available to the conquered Indians, except that provided by a few missionaries of the Italian Catholic congregation of Giovanni Bosco and the summary preparation for baptism offered by some Catholic parishes to the women and children given to Buenos Aires families.[37] In brief, the policies implemented converged on a single goal: to eliminate the aborigines in order to direct new European immigrants to the exploitation of interior lands.

Therefore, in the late 1880s, blacks and Indians became insignificant minorities and immigration became a major social issue. European scientific racism had laid the groundwork for a way of thinking about race that ended up being applied to ethnicity in the debate on European immigrants, Italians or Russian Jews. This happened despite the fact that Argentinean racial theoreticians had not applied the theory to the immigrants, whom they considered as a whole beneficial to the country.

The nature of immigration evolved as a consequence of two factors: worsening socioeconomic conditions in Europe and the new demand for Argentinean cereals and meat. As the whitening and the modernization of Argentina progressed, it became necessary to attract cheap European laborers rather than educated individuals. The unskilled worker and the poor peasant came to outnumber the artisan, the technician, the merchant, and the teacher.

The melting into Argentina of the newcomers did not happen at the anticipated pace, and the expected intermarriage of immigrants and Argentineans did not take place on a large scale.[38] Furthermore, the immigrants' tendency to refuse naturalization and to form separate communities with mutual benefit societies, cooperative saving banks, national celebrations, schools, and hospitals began to irritate Argentineans.

Although Argentinean society peacefully received the tens of thousands of immigrants disembarking each year, it showed some resistance, particularly noticeable in the reaction of the landed elite. If they were ready to welcome cheap laborers, they also resisted the creation of new social groups, such as foreign-born well-to-do farmers, urban middle classes, and organized proletarians. Their resentment appeared, for example, in the bloody repression of the Swiss and German immigrant farmers' revolt in the province of Santa Fé in 1893. In the cities, principally in Buenos Aires, discrimination against the prosperous immigrants, labeled as nouveaux riches without social skills, was common in selective clubs. However, the most challenging side effect of European immigration for the Argentinean elite was the introduction into Argentina of the new ideologies of socialism and anarchism as well as of trade unionism, in which Italians, Germans, and Russian Jews were especially active. As social unrest grew and strikes multiplied, members of the Argentinean ruling class blamed the faulty political and ethnic selection of the immigrants.[39]

From 1900 onward, Argentinean nationalism revived; it peaked during the celebration of the centennial of independence in 1910. Nationalism led to the formulation of a positive image of the native Argentinean and to the resultant depreciation of the immigrant and was expressed in two ways: constructively through the development of a nationalist education; destructively through xenophobia. As for the former, although Sarmiento in the 1880s had been a precursor of this movement in his campaign against the private schools of the Italian community, neither Ingenieros, himself an Italian immigrant, nor most racist theoreticians took part in it.[40] Bunge did contribute to it with a patriotic textbook.[41]

The leaders of the nationalist educational movement were writer Ricardo Rojas (1882–1957) and physician and writer José María Ramos Mejía (1849–1914). Their reaction did not mean a condemnation of past immigration policy, but a change in priorities: now that Argentina had become a nation of European stock, the next step was to create Argentinean nationalism and culture. As immigration had been the panacea for the country's problems during the nineteenth century, by 1910 it was being replaced by education. It was argued that only through compulsory public education—which stressed patriotism, Spanish language and heritage, national history and geography along with civics—could both the rural areas and the immigrants be integrated into the supposedly true Argentina. The search for a common and distinctive past ironically led to the Indians' rehabilitation or, more precisely, to a romantic tellurism including the presence of the "Indian soul."[42] Simultaneously, criticism of foreign schools resumed, the main target this time being the Jewish schools of the province of Entre-Ríos.[43]

As for xenophobia, and especially anti-Semitism, the Catholic church actively incited it as a way to recapture its dominant position within society. Clerical and Catholic writers defined the truly Argentinean values as Catholicism, Latinity, paternalism, family, and order. This definition pointed clearly to anarchists, socialists, and Russian Jewish immigrants as the homeland's enemies.[44] After the triumph of the Russian Revolution, Russian Jews were commonly suspected of Bolshevism. They also represented an easy target, being the most visible, poor, and defenseless, as well as fitting into the anti-Semitism of the Spanish and Catholic tradition.

Novels and plays popularized a negative image of the immigrant: a parasite living at the expense of the Argentineans, a dishonest tradesman, or a pimp. Buenos Aires' increasing crime, prostitution, vagrancy, and alcoholism began to be blamed on the immigrants.[45] Eventually, nationalism and xenophobia helped to pass the Residence Law of 1902 and the Social Defense Law of 1910, which restricted the immigration of "undesirable elements" and allowed the expulsion of foreign "agitators."

Ethnic prejudice combined with class antagonism to provoke further violence. When workers' unions announced a general strike in Buenos Aires to coincide with the centennial celebrations of 1910, resistance became brutal. A state of siege was declared. Young members of the Creole elite formed groups to sack anarchist, socialist, and Jewish centers. In 1919, again as a consequence of another general strike, young armed Creoles encouraged by the church joined the police in "self-defense" squads. Shouting anti-Semitic and antianarchist slogans, they fell upon the mainly Russian Jewish working-class sector of the capital. The exact balance of the so-called Semana Trágica was never known, but estimates range from sixty-five to a thousand dead, most of the victims Russian Jews.[46]

Slowly but surely, by 1920 the patterns of Argentinean nationalism were fixed until the advent of Peronism. They included the reassertion of the value of the Hispanic ethnic and cultural component as well as of the Catholic faith in the native population, a reassertion that was made at the expense of foreigners, especially anarchists and Russian Jews. In sum, Sarmiento, Bunge, and Ingenieros made their racial thinking conform to European scientific racism, although they all moved away from it by attaching a fundamental importance to education as a way to divert biological determinism. While they focused their writing on the "colored" races, Argentina was becoming a nation of mainly Creoles and European immigrants. The composition of the country had little relationship with their theories. However, these theories helped to sustain the policies of exclusion of the Indians, as well as the choice of education as the means of unifying the nation. They also contributed to making an issue of race and ethnicity in the debates on nationalism, but they had no direct influence on its patterns.

Racial Thought in Cuba: The Refusal of the African Component

After independence, Cuba's Creole elite, surprisingly, followed Argentina's model of nation building, despite great differences in racial makeup. The ruling class chose to reinforce the Hispanic component of the population through immigration rather than to unify the new nation. According to the census of 1899, Cuba had a population of 1,573,000: approximately 66 percent whites, 33 percent Afro-Cubans, and one percent Chinese.[47] The proportion of blacks had been diminishing since the end of slave trade in the 1860s, a trend that the elite hoped to strengthen through massive Spanish immigration and further intermarriage.

However, Cuba had many qualities that could have led to a different project of nation building. Both the "race of color" (as blacks and mulattoes were then called in Cuba) and Creoles had participated side-by-side in the struggle against Spain not only as soldiers, but also as commanders and propagandists. Cuba's leader of the independence movement, José Martí (1853–1895), was a militant antiracist and defended Cuban racial fraternity, professing that "Cuban means more than white, more than mulatto, more than black."[48] In addition, as early as the 1880s, an Afro-Cuban intelligentsia organized without challenging the system. It created associations in the country and in exile that promoted instruction, culture, and morals among the "race of color."[49]

The Afro-Cuban intellectuals, nevertheless, were not sufficiently strong to warrant the recognition of the Creole elite. Because of the death in the war of José Martí and of the mulatto general Antonio Maceo (1845–1896), they lost their most powerful spokesmen. Even if the United States had not occupied Cuba after the Spanish Cuban American War and implemented some segregationist policies, there is little doubt that the Creole elite was not ready to share power with the Afro-Cubans after independence.[50] The official anthropological study made in 1900 of Maceo's skeleton is revealing of that attitude. After stating the inferiority of the mulatto, except when the white element dominated in the "cross-breeding," the commission decided that, whereas Maceo's skeleton testified to his black origin, his skull definitely approximated one of the white race. The commission concluded that, "given the race to which he belonged, the environment in which he conducted his activities, ANTONIO MACEO can be considered as a *truly superior man*."[51]

Race was indeed an omnipresent theme in the writing of the Cuban Creole elite of the early twentieth century.[52] I shall focus here on two intellectuals: Francisco Figueras and Fernando Ortiz Fernández. Although he is almost forgotten today, politician Francisco Figueras (b. 1853) wrote in 1907 an unusual global interpretation of Cuba's problems—the inspired-by-Bunge *Cuba y su evolución colonial*—which made a deep impression on Creole intellectuals and literate audiences and became a reference for other writers. Fernando Ortiz (1881–1969) is well known as the first Cuban ethnologist and as an antiracist, but he is less recognized for his pre–World War II positivism and interest in criminology.

After studying Cubans' ethnic composition, psychology, and way of life, Figueras tried to prove their racial incapacity to form an independent republic. For him, Cubans were still in the process of "formation," but already a physical type close to that of the Spaniard, slightly shorter than the average European, well proportioned, and brachycephalic. The color of their skin was "matte olive," but as they lived in the tropical zone where the sun produced intense alterations, their "color was to be an element of little importance in the determination of the *limpieza de sangre*."[53] Cubans, said Figueras, were the result of intermarriage between the Siboney Indians, the black Africans, the various dwellers of peninsular Spain and the Canary Islands, the French of Haiti and Louisiana, and the Spanish Creoles of Florida. The effeminate and docile Indians were in a degenerative stage leading inevitably to their extinction when the Spaniards conquered them and "fulfilled that sentence."[54] Thus they left little influence on Cuban society. The "even more inferior" blacks replaced them.[55] A race vegetating in childhood, the Africans brought to Cuba their musical sense, their exhibitionism and lasciviousness, and their lack of foresight.[56]

As for the Spaniards, they contributed to the Cuban character with their perspicacity and intelligence, their imagination and hospitality. However, their contempt for women produced sexual immorality. Likewise, two of their institutions were largely responsible for Cuban stagnation: an education based on feelings, "this quality that we share with inferior beings,"[57] and slavery, which poisoned social life and condemned the slave, whatever his or her race, to viciousness. Thus the Spaniards were unable to bring civilization (understood by Figueras as capitalist modernization, especially work habits and enterprise) to Cuba. Civilization began only with the British occupation of Havana in 1762, followed by the French emigration from Louisiana and Haiti around 1800, and finally the American military occupation in 1898 and 1906. Climate and environment had also been decisive in determining Cubans' high-strung quality and reinforcing their disdain for work. In brief, Figueras attributed 75 percent of Cuban national traits to the Spaniards, 10 percent to the Africans, and 15 percent to the "Cubans" themselves.[58]

According to Figueras, natural selection would eventually lead to the absorption of the blacks by the superior race, but it was a long-term evolution slowed by the persistence of an important nucleus of self-reproducing blacks. Their percentage in the society was diminishing mainly because they intermarried with whites, but not without imposing their physical and psychological traits on the latter. This explained why an attentive observer could find apparently white Cubans with "impudent prognatism" and "capricious hair waves," or who were the parents of "a child of such singular features and disproportionate members" that he or she testified to "the missing step in the zoological chain . . . between man and gorilla."[59]

Cuba could not be saved without strengthening its links with the United States and without an Anglo-Saxon education based on reason. Physical and moral health

"Rehabilitation" of Indians through agricultural labor: Matacos in the canefields of Chaco, Argentina, 1917. Photo courtesy of the Archivo General de la Nación, Argentina.

NUMERO 9.   Habana 14 de Julio de 1912.   5 CENTAVOS

LA BROMA

Semanario Político con Caricaturas.–Redacción y Administración Cuba Nº 1
Teléfono A 8361.

ACOGIDO A LA FRANQUICIA POSTAL, Y REGISTRADO COMO CORRESPONDENCIA DE SEGUNDA CLASE.

PRESIDENCIA

¡SIEMPRE LO MISMO.....!

¡Por cumplir con su deber
Presidente quiere ser!

Cover of a satirical magazine portraying the general in charge of repressing
the Partido Independiente de Color in Oriente, 1912. Courtesy of Biblioteca
Nacional José Martí, Havana.

Club "Guerrilla de Maceo," a proindependence, Afro-Cuban association, Cuba, 1890s. Photo courtesy of Biblioteca Nacional José Martí, Havana.

should also be promoted, for it could counter the deleterious effects of race. Yet, as Figueras was getting rid of the blacks in the evolutionary process, he focused on the practical training of the Creole women, mothers of tomorrow's Cuban.[60]

A discussion of Ortiz here may at first seem surprising. As early as the 1900s, he denounced the concept of race as unscientific, "nothing more than a grouping of beings according to determined differential points of view" (the color of the skin, the facial angle, and so on). He preferred to deal with a more dynamic concept of civilization, one that accounted for humanity's progress. Like other positivists, he believed in the inevitability of the Anglo-Saxon model of civilization, but also in the ability of any race to embrace that model.[61] These statements aside, however, Ortiz' analysis of Cuban components did not fundamentally differ from a racial one: he saw in the three races—white, black, and yellow, each with its own psychological character—the basic explanation of the still not fully formed Cuban type.[62] Not surprisingly, among his notes for a projected but never written "sociología cubana" figured Sarmiento, Bunge, and Ingenieros.[63] His contribution to Latin American thought was mainly to integrate the criminology of Italian physician Cesare Lombroso with racial theory about Cuba and to focus on the cultural manifestations of races rather than on their physical features.

Ortiz considered triracial Cuba to be a good laboratory for a differential study of delinquency, especially among blacks. For him, Africans were inferior "because of their lack of integral civilization" and morals. They were lascivious lovers, given to polygamy, and had no cohesive families; their religion led them to human sacrifice, anthropophagy, and the most brutal superstitions.[64] Thus their criminality differed from the white criminality theorized by Lombroso, who saw it as an individual form of atavism in which the criminal showed an ancestral moral primitiveness in an otherwise fully developed psyche. The criminality of the Africans, Ortiz said, was explained by the complete primitiveness of their collective psyche, incapable of moral discernment. Consequently, those who were taken to Cuba could not adjust to the higher Spanish civilization, and "the whole race entered into a bad life [*mala vida*]."[65] Cuban criminality was therefore predominantly shaped by them and influenced by African superstitions, organizations, languages, and dances, as were Cuban witchcraft and fetishism: "Today Cuban society psychically evolves in an imperceptible graduation from the white, who is placed by his talents at the level of the refined civilized man, to the African black who, sent back to his native country, would resume his libations in the open skull of an enemy."[66] The gap between the two races was narrowing, however, as some blacks were acquiring culture, while the white lower class was Africanizing its way of life.

What solution, then, did Ortiz propose in order to bring progress to Cuba? Not the disappearance of the blacks through natural death, intermarriage, or massive white immigration, but the elimination of the manifestations of African culture as stereotyped by him. In fact, as an ethnologist, he wanted to eradicate those traits, but not without having previously studied them, keeping the most representative in a museum of folklore.

Widespread scientific education and U.S. influence were to play an important role in that campaign. Ortiz, mentioning the positive effect Methodism had on North American blacks, even thought of importing "more progressive" religions to eliminate fetishism.[67] Besides, it was urgent to "destroy the infectious focus" by adequately repressing witches, healers, and other spreaders of primitiveness through a modern penitentiary system. Laws should be revised so that witchcraft, even without otherwise criminal actions, would be illegal. Immigration of blacks should continue to be avoided, as they would bring new elements of backwardness. Ortiz counted also on the good example of "those colored individuals who, thanks to their intelligence and morality, ascended to a level superior to that of the majority of their race" and on the generally better conditions of Cuban blacks as compared to those in the rest of America.[68]

Although some of his contemporaries considered Figueras a reactionary, Ortiz belonged to the progressive line of the Liberals. Nevertheless, both, basing their assertions on colonial and nineteenth-century sources, perpetuated a negative image of the Afro-Cuban. Crime, prostitution, ignorance, and poverty were partially explained by racial theories. In addition, the century-long specter of Haiti's black revolution against whites was raised again by the Creole elite in order to prevent any change in the social structure.

White Policies and Black Responses in Cuba

As for Cuban social policy, two major concessions were made to nonwhites: the Constitution of 1901 gave them equality (without specifying race, sex, place of birth, or religion) and universal male suffrage. But no program was designed to help those freed from slavery as recently as 1886. Ethnic cultural disparities were considerable at the turn of the century: approximately 50 percent of whites were literate, compared to only 28 percent of blacks and mulattoes. Nevertheless, the importance conferred by the American military administration of 1899–1902 on public education was not continued by the first Cuban governments. The public school system, from primary education to university, was certainly not segregated, but racial discrimination operated on the secondary level, in which the great majority of *colegios* were private and refused nonwhite students on racial or economic grounds. Thus, although the percentage of literate blacks grew to 53 by 1919, it was still difficult for a black or a mulatto to enter Havana National University.[69]

Many policies directly aimed at segregating blacks. Illegal racial discrimination in clubs, restaurants, and public parks was not officially opposed. Segregation was even applied to presidential receptions held during Tomás Estrada Palma's tenure in 1902 and 1905, to which the wives of the only black senator and of two black congressmen were not invited.[70] Racial discrimination in the army had been initiated by the U.S. administration. In 1899, it dissolved the revolutionary army, in which blacks and mulattoes were overrepresented, and replaced it with a white-commanded Rural Guard. By doing so, it robbed Afro-Cuban men of the principal channel of upward social mobility for non-Creoles existing after independence in most of Hispanic America. This policy was carefully continued by Creole governments anxious to prevent any insurrection like that in Haiti. Through a system of promotion based on political recommendation rather than on professional criteria, they succeeded in having an all-Creole command and in keeping blacks and mulattoes at the lower ranks of sergeant and corporal.[71] The Creole elite also avoided nominating Afro-Cubans to provincial or national office and would not place them in the Havana police. Significantly, too, blacks and mulattoes were excluded from the diplomatic staff. Although political parties needed their vote, they were reluctant to let them run for office.

Moreover, the immigration law imposed on Cuba by the United States in 1902, which prohibited Chinese immigration and restricted that of nonwhites, was strengthened by the Law of Immigration and Colonization of 1906. The new legislation encouraged the settlement of families from Europe and the Canary Islands, as well as the immigration of day laborers from Sweden, Norway, Denmark, and northern Italy.[72]

The Creole elite greeted the further decline of the black population to 30 percent together with the growth of the total population counted in the census of 1907 as signs of progress accompanying the rapid increase of production and trade. The disappearance of yellow fever was also thought to be beneficial to the whitening of the island. In 1900, a professor of intertropical pathology at Havana University, Juan Guiteras, deplored the supposedly lower resistance of Creole children to yellow fever as compared to the blacks and asserted that "in order to achieve white racial preponderance in the Caribbean, it is necessary to solve the problem of yellow fever."[73] In 1913, he exultantly announced that, since the medical victory over the disease, Cuba's white mortality had dropped, while black mortality due to socioeconomic factors was still high. In his view, this proved the error of the theory on tropical inferiority: "The tropical climate is compatible with the highest expressions of human activity. . . . The white race's acclimatization to the tropics has been a complete success."[74] Furthermore, the ideal of whitening was so strong among the Creole elite families that intermarriage of one of their members with an Afro-Cuban would have been considered an outrage. Personal relationship between them and blacks was still mostly one of masters and servants.[75]

As a result, after independence Afro-Cuban intellectuals faced the difficult task of destroying the image of the uncivilized black and claiming their rightful share in the new society. Blacks did not enter into the racial debate except to differentiate the Afro-Cubans from the primitive Africans,[76] but they contributed to the discussion of integration. Some advocated the discreet individual progress of the "race of color" within the established system through merit, education, and work, so that they would eventually become unnoticed in a predominantly white society.[77] Others believed in more collective solutions to discrimination, albeit ones that would not challenge the social order.[78] Rafael Serra (1858–1909), Martí's black companion in New York, turned away from the ideals of racial unity to propose the development of a black Cuban bourgeoisie and the creation of separate organizations to defend the rights and interests of the "class of color."[79]

In reality, resentment and radicalization were rapidly growing among a new generation of Afro-Cuban nationalists not ready to hold back their claims to justice in the name of Cuban unity. After the elections of August 1908, in which no blacks were elected, one of them, Evaristo Estenoz, decided that it was time for the Afro-Cubans to have their own political party, so he created the Partido Independiente de Color. Its program contemplated popular demands designed for integrating the "class of color," such as compulsory free education from eight to fourteen years, free technical, secondary, and university education, state control of private schools, abolition of the death penalty, reform of the judicial and penitentiary systems, and the eight-hour work day. It also advocated an end to racial discrimination, priority for Cubans in employment, black access to higher positions in public service and the diplomatic corps, and an end to the ban on nonwhite immigration.[80]

The Partido Independiente de Color saw its membership rapidly increase and claimed 60,000 members in 1910. They openly threatened the two established parties. From the beginning the political establishment accused the Independientes de Color of racism, on grounds that they were mobilizing blacks against whites. They were often harassed, and some, including Estenoz, were sentenced to short imprisonments. In April 1910, over 220 Independientes and suspects were arrested throughout the island for alleged conspiracy and rebellion against the elected government.[81] Simultaneously, an amendment to the Electoral Law was passed that prohibited political parties representing one particular race.[82] Thus, the Partido Independiente de Color was outlawed, and Estenoz and most leaders of the movement remained in custody for several months. Later, all were freed after trial and campaigned unsuccessfully for the suppression of the electoral amendment. In May 1912, they organized an armed protest, principally in the province of Oriente, where Afro-Cubans, more numerous, were also suffering from losses of land. The government repression was bloody: in two months, between three thousand and four thousand Afro-Cubans, including Estenoz, were massacred by the army and zealous volunteers.[83]

Creole interpretations of the slaughter were significant. Two journalists who followed the army saw the "Guerrita del 12" (the Little War of 1912) as a chapter in the "perpetual and implacable struggle between races" that never could mix. They warned against any black rebellions and advocated the creation of a national secret police and militias based on the U.S. model.[84] The prestigious journal *Cuba Contemporánea* published an article by Carlos de Velasco, who imputed Afro-Cubans' difficulties to their lack of preparation—"It is necessary that each one knows his place"—and argued that the Creole elite should continue to run the country. José Antonio Saco's solutions were considered the most valid: massive white immigration and total prohibition of black immigration.[85]

Afro-Cubans were stunned and divided. The black congressmen signed a manifesto in July 1912 that denied the existence of racial discrimination in Cuba and called for national unity. In 1915, journalist Ramón Vasconcelos initiated in the Liberal newspaper *La Prensa* a section called "Palpitaciones de la raza de color" (pulse of the race of color), in which both black and nonblack essayists discussed the social problem of Afro-Cubans. Afro-Cuban intellectuals, professionals, artists, and other members of the middle class gathered after 1917 in the Club Atenas, where they tried to play a role similar to that of the NAACP in the United States. Culturally closer to the Creole elite than to the "class of color," they did not truly represent the interests of Afro-Cuban people. The massacre of 1912 indeed dealt a fatal blow to Afro-Cuban organization on ethnic lines. Furthermore, many signs seem to point to its being a planned racist repression aimed at terrifying blacks and mulattoes and at keeping them out of politics and power.[86]

After 1912, racism directed at Afro-Cubans used new expedients such as the struggle against witchcraft and against Haitian and Jamaican immigration. African witchcraft had been stigmatized first by Ortiz, whose work became a standard reference on the matter. However, many maintained that the death penalty was the only way to eradicate the evil. The decades of 1910 and 1920 saw a collective hysteria, often stimulated by the press, based on stories of actual or imaginary black witchcraft and of little white girls mysteriously disappearing during the preparation of magical potions. Any sign of witchcraft could end with imprisonment. African drums, carnivals, and dance were prohibited. A few Afro-Cuban "witches" were lynched, and some newspapers praised these occurrences as a progressive manifestation of Cubans' North Americanization.[87]

The racist dimension is best illustrated by changing immigration policy. After independence, Spaniards who settled in Cuba enjoyed the protection of the U.S. military government and did not lose their land or properties. Encouraged by Cuban authorities, approximately 900,000 Spaniards and Canary Islanders emigrated to Cuba between 1900 and 1929, enabling this community to strengthen its position in trade and industry. In contrast to the Argentinean elite's view of immigrants, these immigrants did not incur hostility from a Creole upper class busy with well-paid government positions. The few protests against the Spanish presence were directed toward their lack of obedience to Cuban laws or to the increasing number of Spanish clergy in private education.[88]

Creole resentment focused on Afro-Caribbean and Chinese immigration. Beginning in 1900, sugar planters lobbied for a new immigration law that would allow cheap seasonal labor for the harvest. By the end of 1912, the first contingent of 1,400 Haitians arrived in Oriente. Until 1927, an estimated 150,000 Haitians and Jamaicans migrated to Cuba, a small figure compared to the Spaniards, especially because most of them, unlike the Spaniards, returned to their home island after the crop.[89] Nevertheless, Creole intellectuals became alarmed. Their most common arguments were that Haitians would bring about revolution or racial war in Cuba, and that Afro-Caribbean immigration reversed the Cuban process of ethnic evolution toward a predominantly white population.[90] Haitians and Jamaicans became the scapegoat for many Cuban problems, as well as easy prey for unscrupulous employers, racist policemen, rural guards, and witch hunters.

Afro-Cuban associations such as the Club Atenas protested these new and subtle expressions of racism.[91] However, manifestations of African culture, such as dance, carnival, and healing, contradicted their own project of Afro-Cuban integration into "white civilization." Furthermore, Caribbean immigrants competed with Afro-Cuban labor by accepting lower wages. Thus it was difficult for black intellectuals to present airtight counterarguments to the Creole elite.

When writing about race, then, Cuban Creole intellectuals harmonized with the framework of European scientific racism. Although Cuba had a high proportion of blacks and mulattoes in its population, most intellectuals hoped that these ethnic sections would eventually give way to the whites, or at least, according to Ortiz, become civilized by giving up African culture. As was the case in Argentina, European immigration and education were to play an important part in this process. Spanish immigration was indeed implemented, together with racial segregation. However, groups of black intellectuals organized to achieve integration. Others founded a popular party of color and ended up in a rebellion that was put down in a slaughter. By the 1920s, Creole intellectuals had resigned themselves to the fact that Cuba would remain a biracial society. But they continued to favor the Hispanic component, allowing only a few expressions of Afro-Cuban culture. Segregation did not disappear and most open racism was turned against a new scapegoat: the black Haitian and Jamaican immigrants.

A Comparative Perspective: Scientific Racism, Social Reality, and the Intellectual

Thus Argentina and Cuba are two countries in which, after independence, the Creole elite decided to build a predominantly white nation by means of massive European immigration. By 1930, for reasons beyond the focus of this study, Argentina had succeeded and Cuba had failed. In both cases, the labor market together with the intellectuals or the policymakers determined who was to immigrate: some trained North Europeans, but principally unskilled South Europeans in Argentina; Spaniards, but also Afro-Caribbeans in Cuba. Not surprisingly, in both cases, Creole popular discontent fell on the least threatening but most visible immigrant: the Russian Jew in Argentina and the Haitian or Jamaican black in Cuba. In both countries, nationality as defined by European nineteenth-century nationalism became a dominant issue, and education was singled out as its most efficient shaper.

The analogies cannot be carried further. After Argentina had evicted or exterminated nonwhites, some of its intellectuals worked hard to integrate Latin immigrants into a newly created Argentinean culture that was a complex combination of Spanish language, Hispanic tradition, Catholicism, Argentinean history, and even romantic tellurism rehabilitating the mestizo gaucho and the savage Indian. As Europeanization had needed the Indian and the gaucho as the "other" against whom civilization struggled, nationalism was to be built as a bulwark against the anarchist, the socialist, and the Jew. The irony of Argentinean nationalism and racism is that in reality it was very close to the European model: a search for a mystical past, in which the Spanish conqueror and the independent gaucho replaced the Aryan peasant and warrior freeman in fighting the identical enemy.

Cuba's independence could not have been a greater illusion, and not only because of U.S. occupations. No sooner had the Creole elite cut the bonds with Spain than it called for the continuation of Spanish immigration and neglected to nationalize colonial Spaniards' properties. Although that policy may have limited growing U.S. imperialism, it was principally aimed at reducing blacks' and mulattoes' participation in the Cuban nation. Nevertheless, Cuba remained a biracial society and its intelligentsia attempted to cope with that reality. The African heritage was not acknowledged as a whole, nor as a constructive component of a still very Hispanic Cuban culture. Only those elements that generated money and votes, such as music, divination, nonritual dance, and organized carnival, were eventually allowed.[92]

One of the most striking features of Argentinean and Cuban scientific racism was its relationship with society. In both cases, white supremacy was attractive not only to the ruling elite, but to some larger sectors such as the nascent Creole middle class. However, the criticism of miscegenation and the theory of Anglo-Saxon superiority over Latins that formed part of European scientific racism raised too many questions about Hispanic America's future to be sustained over the long term, even by the Creole elite. From Argentina's and Cuba's experiences, it appears that the Creole elite was inspired by racial theories especially during the first stage of modernization. For example, it set up a program of European immigration based on these views. Scientific racism was also used to justify some of the most violent policies against ethnic minorities, such as the wars of Indian extermination. Furthermore, it was a component within the positivistic protest against the ideological domination of the Catholic church, against which could be placed the model of Anglo-Saxon Protestant materialism.

However, when scientific racism threatened ruling class interests, it was quick to distance itself from this doctrine. This was obvious in the case of Argentina with regard to the reaction of the Creole landed elite to "undesirable" European immigrants: it was not only Russian Jews who were expelled, but also some Spaniards and Germans. In the case of Cuba, absolute consistency with scientific racism should have favored annexation to the superior Anglo-Saxon United States; that was not the conclusion of the Cuban elite. As well, Creole landowners in Cuba eventually won out over the racially sustained opposition to their demand for cheap Afro-Caribbean labor.

This is not to say, of course, that racial prejudice vanished, but only that strict scientific racism could be adapted to fit particular socioeconomic situations. Some assertions included in the global theory could be deliberately omitted in favor of others more applicable to the specific situation—in the case of the Afro-Caribbean laborers, their supposed stamina and resistance to the tropical climate.

An important aspect of the relationship between racial thought and social structure is the acceptance of scientific racism in the nascent progressive circles of Latin America. The examples of Ingenieros and Ortiz, both criminologists, indicate that some parallels could be drawn with contemporary Italy—where criminology was part of a progressive movement aimed at building a more peaceful society—and with some deterministic currents of socialism. In the case of Ingenieros, it is striking that his white Argentinean pride and outspoken racism did not face major opposition from the politically advanced intelligentsia of the rest of Latin America, although he was the only Argentinean openly relating human evolution to complexion (progressing from the darkest to the lightest) as well as the only one standing for black slavery. Instead, Ingenieros was widely admired as a socialist and an inspirer of youth beginning with his support for the movement for university reform in Córdoba in 1918. His contemporaries emphasized his abundant writing on morals, philosophy, and sociology, as well as his struggle to improve the judicial system's approach to crime, but ignored his visceral antiblack feelings. Similarly, Ortiz was praised for his minute descriptions of Afro-Cuban slavery and witchcraft, but was not opposed for the racist argument of some of his interpretations.

It should also be mentioned that Alberdi's *Bases* still inspired the program for European peasant immigration that the Socialist party of Argentina proposed in order to civilize the Argentinean countryside.[93] Although outspoken racism vanished in the late 1920s, the racist message of many authors probably did not personally offend progressive intellectuals and students, who at the time were mainly Creoles. In fact, antiracism did not become an active and important part of Latin American progressive thought until World War II, when it was launched by prominent Europeans and North Americans and when Latin American minorities expressed themselves more frequently through writing.

When looking at Argentinean and Cuban thinkers on race in a broader perspective,[94] one is disconcerted by their acceptance of European racial theories. In countries where science did not have a long tradition, intellectuals chose psychobiology, rather than socioeconomic analysis, and heredity rather than environment, to account for their national problems. Their choice was not a blind one as, at the beginning of the twentieth century, cultural environmentalism, sociology, and Marxism were already influential in Europe.

Their writings were a pale and often ill-digested adaptation of European and North American works on race, psychobiology and history in which social Darwinist and positivist interpretations prevailed. Like their mentors, they abstained from presenting evidence or data. No field research or thorough direct observation of Argentina's or Cuba's society that might have questioned European theories, notably on intermarriage, supported their works. They sidestepped the difficulty of passing for scientists by evading fundamental contradictions or by using scientific metaphors.[95] However, their effort to appear scientific was wasted, as their audience was ready to believe racism anyway. Because their ideas meshed with the racist trends of European and North American social thought that had inspired them, their books were in turn used by foreign theoreticians as evidence to confirm racial prejudices concerning Latin America. In short, they had trapped themselves in a vicious circle of racist thought.

Even within the framework of scientific racism, until 1930, very little autonomy among intellectuals was noticeable, even though Latin American reality so apparently contradicted European ideas. No one dared or wanted to oppose seriously the concept of race. All accepted the established three or four "fundamental races" and their supposed characteristics. While the context blurred the limits fixed between races, intellectuals searched for explanations in the stereotypes attached to the so-called original races in order to prognosticate the features and traits of a not-yet-formed "national type." Multiracial and multicultural nations were beyond their perspective.

They undertook only some mild re-theoretization in order to avoid total pessimism. The most important innovation was the role they unanimously, from Sarmiento to Ortiz, conferred on Anglo-Saxon practical education as a way to correct heredity, thus getting away from the influence of the most intransigent racism. Argentinean and Cuban theoreticians also tried to modify racial classification in minor ways. The main colonial castes, such as the mulatto, the mestizo, and the zambo (of black and Indian descent), were too firmly established as racial categories to be treated as merely transitory, as in some European theories. Figueras, to include more Cubans in the white race, wrote that in the sunny tropics the color of the skin was not a decisive element in the determination of race and predicted that the future Cuban type would be a "matte olive" European. Ingenieros reassured himself with the idea of belonging to a European(ized) nation, as he asserted the equality within the white race and the biological success of whitening through miscegenation. Ortiz went as far as to exchange theoretically the biological definition of race for a cultural one.

These modifications, except as regards the role of education, were not very significant, as they did not attenuate the racist framework of thinking. Despite his cultural definition of race, Ortiz could not shake off European stereotypes when he built his theory of Afro-Cuban criminality. Moreover, reflection on intermarriage never led Argentinean and particularly Cuban Creole intellectuals to a firm reassertion of the value of miscegenation—in the sense of the "cosmic race" of Mexican philosopher José Vasconcelos. They all expressed doubts about the psychological balance of the mulatto or the mestizo. Many were torn between the hope of whitening through intermarriage and the fear that the "bad" characteristics of the "lower" races would show up at some stage. More than any other, Bunge worked hard to adapt reality to scientific racism, as his curious attempt to classify Latin American intermarriage shows: he labeled it "hybridism" when it involved Indians and Spaniards and miscegenation when it involved blacks and Spaniards, and he believed that the mixing of Chinese, Africans, and Indians with each other would produce a sterile type. He was constantly struggling between racial prejudice and nationalism. While condemning the supposedly atavistic resurgence of the lower races' characteristics in the process of whitening, he nevertheless predicted that the as-yet unachieved Argentinean physical type was to be white.

Ultimately, then, the difficult relationship between scientific racism and social environment brings up the question of the audience. For whom were Hispanic American intellectuals writing? For their fellow countrymen in order to redeem them, as they claimed? Or for European colleagues, in order to be published in their journals and welcomed in their circles? Or for themselves, to relieve anxiety and guilt? The last hypothesis seems most likely. They tried to build up an imaginary and stereotyped world that would function according to permanent and logical biopsychological laws. It would be a world with acknowledged enemies and myths. A "scientific," "rational" world, when a confusing and rapidly changing reality made it too difficult to find one's identity.

Notes

I would like to thank the Swiss National Fund for Scientific Research for providing the fellowship that made this research possible, as well as Sandra Lauderdale Graham and Della Sprager for their much appreciated comments.

1. On Latin American social thought, see, for example, E. Bradford Burns, *The Poverty of Progress: Latin America in the Nineteenth Century* (Berkeley: University of California Press, 1980); William Rex Crawford, *A Century of Latin American Thought* (Cambridge, Mass.: Harvard University Press, 1961); Miguel Jorrín and John D. Martz, *Latin American Political Thought and Ideology* (Chapel Hill: University of North Carolina Press, 1970); Thomas E. Skidmore, *Black into White: Race and Nationality in Brazilian Thought* (New York: Oxford University Press, 1974); Martin S. Stabb, *In Quest of Identity: Patterns in the Spanish American Essay of Ideas, 1890–1960* (Chapel Hill: University of North Carolina Press, 1967); Ralph Lee Woodward, Jr., ed., *Positivism in Latin America, 1850–1900: Are Order and Progress Reconciliable?* (Lexington, Mass.: D. C. Heath & Co., 1971); and Alberto Zum Felde, *Indice crítico de la literatura hispanoamericana*, 2 vols. (Mexico City: Editorial Guarania, 1954).

2. George M. Fredrickson, *The Black Image in the White Mind: The Debate on Afro-American Character and Destiny, 1817–1914*, 2d ed. (Middletown, Conn.: Wesleyan University Press, 1987), p. xvii.

3. Juan Bautista Alberdi, *Bases y puntos de partida para la organización política de la confederación argentina* (1852; reprint, Buenos Aires: Editorial Plus Ultra, 1981).

4. José Antonio Saco, "La supresión del tráfico de esclavos africanos en la isla de Cuba," in *Colección de papeles científicos, históricos, políticos y de otros ramos sobre la Isla de Cuba ya publicados, ya inéditos*, 3 vols. (Havana: Editorial Lex, 1962), II: 137–154.

5. For example, Augustín E. Alvarez Suárez, *South America; ensayo de psicol-*

ogía política (1894; reprint, Buenos Aires: "La Cultura Argentina," 1918); idem, *La transformación de las razas en América* (Barcelona: F. Granada, 1906); idem, *La herencia moral de los pueblos hispano-americanos* (Buenos Aires: Casa Vaccaro, 1919); Lucas Ayarragaray, "La mestización de las razas en América y sus consecuencias degenerativas," *Revista de Filosofía, Cultura, Ciencias, Educación* 3 (Buenos Aires, 1st sem. 1916): 21–41; idem, *La anarquía argentina y el caudillismo, estudio psicológico de los orígenes argentinos*, 2d ed. (Buenos Aires: J. Lajouane y Cía. Editores, 1925); Carlos Octavio Bunge, *Nuestra América (Ensayo de psicología social)* (1903; reprint, Buenos Aires: Casa Vaccaro, 1918); Juan Agustín García, *La ciudad indiana (Buenos Aires desde 1600 hasta mediados del siglo XVIII)* (Buenos Aires: A. Estrada y Cía., 1900); Joaquín V. González, *La tradición nacional*, 2d ed., in *Obras completas*, 25 vols. (Buenos Aires: Imprenta Mercatali, 1935–1937), XVII: 7–365; José Ingenieros, *Crónicas de viaje, 1905–1906* (1908; reprint, Buenos Aires: R. J. Roggero & Cía., 1951); idem, "La formación de una raza argentina," *Revista de Filosofía, Cultura, Ciencias, Educación* 2 (2nd sem. 1915): 464–483; idem, *Sociología argentina* (1910; reprint, Madrid: D. Jorro Editor, 1913); José María Ramos Mejía, *Las multitudes argentinas. Estudio de psicología colectiva para servir de introducción al libro "Rosas y su tiempo"* (1899; reprint, Buenos Aires: F. Lajouane and Madrid: V. Suárez, 1912); Ricardo Rojas, *La restauración nacionalista; crítica de la educación argentina y bases para una reforma en el estudio de las humanidades modernas* (1909; reprint, Buenos Aires: J. Roldán y Cía., 1922); idem, *Blasón de Plata; meditaciones y evocaciones sobre el abolengo de los argentinos* (Buenos Aires: M. García, 1912); idem, *Eurindia; ensayo de estética fundado en la experiencia histórica de las culturas americanas* (Buenos Aires: J. Roldán y Cía., 1924); Domingo F. Sarmiento, *Conflicto y armonías de las razas en América* (Buenos Aires: S. Ostwald Editor, 1883); idem, *Conflicto y armonía de las razas en América (Conclusiones)* (Mexico City: Universidad Nacional Autónoma de México, 1978); idem, *Condición del extranjero en América*, 2d ed. (Buenos Aires: Librería "La Facultad," 1928); Estanislao S. Zeballos, *Descripción amena de la República argentina*, 2 vols. (Buenos Aires: Imprenta J. Peuser, 1881). One exception is Manuel Ugarte, who was campaigning for Hispanic American unity: *El porvenir de la América Latina, la raza, la integridad territorial y moral, la organización interior* (Valencia: F. Sempere y Cía. Editores, n.d.); idem, *El destino de un continente* (Madrid: Editorial Mundo Latino, 1923); idem, *La patria grande* (Madrid: Editorial Internacional, 1924). On Argentinean positivist thought, see José Luis Romero, *Las ideas políticas en Argentina*, 5th ed. (Buenos Aires: Fondo de Cultura Económica, 1981); and Oscar Terán, *Positivismo y nación en Argentina. Con una selección de textos de J. M. Ramos Mejía, A. Alvarez, C. O. Bunge y José Ingenieros* (Buenos Aires: Puntosur Editores, 1987).

6. The most quoted were Louis Agassiz, James Bryce, Henry Thomas Buckle, Joseph Deniker, Count Arthur de Gobineau, Madison Grant, Ludwig Gumplowicz, Ernst Haeckel, Gustave Le Bon, Friedrich Ratzel, Ernest Renan, Herbert Spencer,

and Hippolyte Taine.

7. Sarmiento, *Conflicto y armonías de las razas en América* (1883), p. 235.

8. Ibid., pp. 14–56, 120, 153, 270. Also his *Conflicto y armonía de las razas en América (Conclusiones)* (1978), p. 16, and "Conferencia leída en el Teatro Nacional después de la muerte de Darwin," in *Cuatro conferencias* (Buenos Aires: W. M. Jackson Editores, n.d.), p. 126.

9. Sarmiento, *Conflicto y armonías* (1883), p. 61, also p. 17.

10. Ibid., pp. 56, 119, 133–137, and *Conflicto y armonía (Conclusiones)* (1978), pp. 16–17.

11. Carlos Octavio Bunge, *Nuestra América*, pp. 41–49, 149–151, 155.

12. See particularly Gustave Le Bon, *Les lois psychologiques de l'évolution des peuples* (1894; reprint, Paris: F. Alcan, 1927).

13. Bunge, *Nuestra América*, pp. 200–202.

14. Ibid., pp. 59–112.

15. Ibid., pp. 136, also 133–135, 167, 182.

16. Ibid., p. 124.

17. For Bunge's analysis of the Indian, see ibid., pp. 121–131, 142.

18. Ibid., pp. 132–146.

19. Ibid., pp. 162–163, 212–213.

20. Ibid., p. 163.

21. Ingenieros, *Crónicas de viaje, 1905–1906*, pp. 190–191; idem, *Sociología argentina*, pp. 11–38, 41, 45; idem, "La formación de una raza argentina," pp. 467–468, 474–475, 478.

22. Ingenieros, *Sociología argentina*, pp. 41, 45.

23. Ingenieros referred to fragments of skull, molar, and femur discovered by Eugene Dubois in Java in 1894, which the naturalist attributed to a hypothetical anthropoid, the *Pithecanthropus erectus*, linking ape to man.

24. Ingenieros, *Crónicas de viaje*, p. 185.

25. Ibid., p. 187.

26. Ibid., p. 188.

27. José Ingenieros, "La simulación en la lucha por la vida en el orden biológico y social," in *Simulación de la locura ante la sociología criminal y la clínica psiquiátrica* (Buenos Aires: Editorial "La Semana Médica," 1903), p. 53.

28. Ingenieros, *Sociología argentina*, pp. 46, 105; idem, *Crónicas*, pp. 221–231; idem, "La formación de una raza argentina," pp. 468–470.

29. Ingenieros, "La formación," p. 477.

30. Ibid., p. 480.

31. Ibid., p. 477, also p. 468.

32. Ingenieros, *Sociología argentina*, p. 100.

33. George Reid Andrews, *The Afro-Argentines of Buenos Aires, 1800–1900* (Madison: University of Wisconsin Press, 1980), p. 4; Haim Avni, *Argentina y la historia de la inmigración judía, 1810–1950* (Buenos Aires & Jerusalem: Editorial Universitaria Magnes-AMIA, 1986), p. 539; Samuel L. Baily, "Marriage Patterns

and Immigrant Assimilation in Buenos Aires, 1882–1923," *Hispanic American Historical Review* 60, no. 1 (February 1980): 36; Angel Rosenblat, *La población indígena y el mestizaje en América*, 2 vols. (Buenos Aires: Editorial Nova, 1954), I: 206–207; James R. Scobie, *Argentina: A City and a Nation* (New York: Oxford University Press, 1964), p. 134. Argentina's total population grew from approximately 1.7 million in 1869 to 7.9 million in 1914 and 11.6 million in 1930.

34. Sarmiento, *Conflicto y armonías*, p. 61; Bunge, *Nuestra América*, pp. 160, 168; José Ingenieros, *La locura en Argentina; locura y brujería en la sociedad colonial, los antiguos "loqueros" de Buenos Aires, los alienados durante la revolución, los alienados en la época de Rosas, los estudios psiquiátricos en la Argentina, los modernos asilos para alienados, censo aproximativo de alienados* (1920; reprint, Buenos Aires: Cooperativa Editora Limitada, 1937), p. 30. See also Andrews, *The Afro-Argentines*, pp. 181–186.

35. Glyn Williams, "Welsh Settlers and Native Americans in Patagonia," *Journal of Latin American Studies* 11, no. 1 (May 1979): 58–62.

36. República Argentina, Congreso Nacional, *Diario de sesiones de la cámara de diputados, año 1879* (Buenos Aires: "La República," 1879), pp. 751–752; *Año 1882* (Buenos Aires: Imprenta de "El Courrier de La Plata," 1882), II: 200–226, 479–480, 531; *Año 1884* (Buenos Aires: Imprenta Stiller y Laas, 1884), I: 934–957.

37. Cayetano Bruno, SBD, *Los salesianos y las hijas de María Auxiliadora en la Argentina* (Buenos Aires: Instituto Salesiano de Artes Gráficas, 1981), I: 257–295; Santiago Luis Copello, *Gestiones del arzobispo Aneiros en favor de los indios hasta la conquista del desierto* (Buenos Aires: Imprenta "Coni," 1945), pp. 174–176.

38. Recent studies demonstrate that, at least until 1900, both Argentineans and foreigners tended to marry within their own group when possible: Samuel L. Baily, "Marriage Patterns," pp. 32–48; Ronald C. Newton, *German Buenos Aires, 1900–1933: Social Change and Cultural Crisis* (Austin: University of Texas Press, 1977), p. 29; Mark D. Szuchman, "The Limits of the Melting Pot in Urban Argentina: Marriage and Integration in Córdoba, 1869–1909," *Hispanic American Historical Review* 57, no. 1 (February 1977): 24–50; and Richard J. Walter, *The Socialist Party of Argentina, 1890–1930* (Austin: University of Texas Press, 1972), p. 4. For a discussion of the issue of immigration, see Tulio Halperín Donghi, "¿Para qué la inmigración? Ideología y política inmigratoria en la Argentina (1810–1914)," in Tulio Halperín Donghi, *El espejo de la historia. Problemas argentinos y perspectivas hispanoamericanas* (Buenos Aires: Editorial Sudamericana, 1987), pp. 189–238.

39. Ezequiel Gallo, *Farmers in Revolt: The Revolution of 1893 in the Province of Santa Fé, Argentina* (London: Athlone Press, 1976), pp. 5–8, 15, 35–51, 62–63, 73–75; Carl Solberg, *Immigration and Nationalism: Argentina and Chile, 1890–1914* (Austin: University of Texas Press, 1970), pp. 80–83, 108–113; Walter, *The Socialist Party*, pp. 48–51, 67–68.

40. Sarmiento, *Condición del extranjero*. See, for example, the writing of physician and historian Lucas Ayarragaray (n. 5).

41. Carlos Octavio Bunge, *Nuestra patria. Libro de lectura para la educación nacional* (Buenos Aires: A. Estrada y Cía. Editores, [1910?]).

42. For example, Ricardo Rojas, *La restauración nacionalista*, and Ramos Mejía, *Las multitudes argentinas*, p. 289.

43. See the journal of the National Superior Board of Education, *El monitor de la educación común*, 1900s and 1910s.

44. See, for example, articles in the Catholic newspaper of Buenos Aires, *El Pueblo*, such as "Los Pilatos" and "Selección inmigratoria" (24 March 1910); also "Dos sinagogas refundidas. Alianza judaico-socialista" (17 November 1918).

45. Julia Kirk Blackwelder and Lyman L. Johnson, "Changing Criminal Patterns in Buenos Aires, 1890 to 1914," *Journal of Latin American Studies* 14, no. 2 (November 1982): 359–380; Judith Laikin Elkin, *Jews of Latin American Republics* (Chapel Hill: University of North Carolina Press, 1980), p. 108; Nora Glickman, "The Image of the Jew in Brazilian and Argentinian Literature" (PhD diss., New York University, 1978), p. 89; Newton, *German Buenos Aires*, p. 24; Eugene F. Sofer, *From Pale to Pampa: A Social History of the Jews of Buenos Aires* (New York: Holmes and Meier, 1982), p. 44; Solberg, *Immigration*, pp. 81–89, 93–101; Szuchman, "The Limits of the Melting Pot," p. 28.

46. Elkin, *Jews*, pp. 58–60, 81–82; Sofer, *From Pale to Pampa*, pp. 36–44; Solberg, *Immigration*, p. 112; Ruth Thompson, "The Limitations of Ideology in the Early Argentine Labour Movement: Anarchism in the Trade Unions, 1890–1920," *Journal of Latin American Studies* 16, no. 1 (May 1984): 87; Walter, *The Socialist Party*, pp. 48–52, 154–155, 168.

47. Or 58 percent native whites, 17 percent mulattoes, 15 percent blacks, 9 percent foreign whites (generally Spaniards), and one percent Chinese. See Census of 1899, in Hortensia Pichardo, *Documentos para la historia de Cuba*, 5 vols. (Havana: Editorial de Ciencias Sociales, 1968–1980), II: 58.

48. José Martí, "Mi raza" (*Patria*, 16 April 1893), in *Obras completas*, 28 vols. (Havana: Editorial Nacional de Cuba, 1963–1973), II: 299.

49. Among them were La Liga, created by Rafael Serra with José Martí in New York, and the Directorio Central de Sociedades de Color, founded by Juan Gualberto Gómez. See Directorio Central de la Raza de Color, *Reglamento del Directorio Central de la Raza de Color* (Havana: Imprenta La Lucha, 1892), pp. 3–6; and Rafael Serra, *Ensayos políticos, sociales y económicos* (New York: Impr. A. W Howes, 1899), p. 145. See also Rebecca Scott, *Slave Emancipation in Cuba: The Transition to Free Labor, 1860–1899* (Princeton: Princeton University Press, 1985), pp. 268–278.

50. See, for example, Manuel de la Cruz, *La revolución cubana y la raza de color (apuntes y datos) por un cubano sin odios* (Key West, Fla.: Imprenta "La Propaganda," 1895).

51. J. R. Montalvo; C. de la Torre; and L. Montané, *El cráneo de Antonio Maceo (Estudio antropológico)* (Havana: Imprenta Militar, 1900), p. 15 (original emphasis).

52. See, for example, Ramón M. Alfonso, *La prostitución en Cuba y especialmente en La Habana* (Havana: Imprenta P. Fernández y Cía., 1902); Rogelio de Armas, "Nuestra población rural y la Liga agraria," *Cuba Contemporánea* 4 (January 1914): 74–87; Raimundo Cabrera, *Cuba y sus jueces; rectificaciones oportunas* (Havana: Imprenta "El Retiro," 1887); idem, "Llamamiento a los cubanos por la Sociedad Económica de Amigos del País," *Revista Bimestre Cubana* 18, no. 2 (March–April 1923): 81–84; Francisco Carrera y Justiz, *El municipio y la cuestión de razas* (Havana: Imprenta la Moderna Poesía, 1904); idem, *El municipio y los extranjeros. Los españoles en Cuba* (Havana: Imprenta la Moderna Poesía, 1904); Miguel de Carrión, "El desenvolvimiento social de Cuba en los últimos veinte años," *Revista Bimestre Cubana* 18, no. 4 (July–August 1923): 313–319, and 18, no. 5 (September–October 1923): 345–364; Francisco Figueras, *La intervención y su política* (Havana: Imprenta Avisador Comercial, 1906); idem, *Cuba y su evolución colonial* (Havana: Imprenta Avisador Comercial, 1907); Ramiro Guerra y Sánchez, *Un cuarto de siglo de evolución cubana* (Havana: Librería "Cervantes," 1924); Mario Guiral Moreno, "Nuestros problemas políticos, económicos y sociales," *Cuba Contemporánea* 5 (August 1914): 401–424; Juan Guiteras, "Estudios demográficos. Aclimatación de la raza blanca en los trópicos," *Revista Bimestre Cubana* 8, no. 2 (November–December 1913): 405–421; Fernando Ortiz [Fernandez], *Hampa afrocubana. Los negros brujos (apuntes para un estudio de etnología criminal)* (1906; reprint, Madrid: Editorial América, [1917?]); idem, *La reconquista de América* (Paris: P. Ollendorff, 1911); idem, *Entre cubanos* (1914[?]; reprint (Havana: Editorial de Ciencias Sociales, 1987); idem, *Hampa afrocubana. Los negros esclavos* (1916; reprint, Havana: Editorial de Ciencias Sociales, 1975); idem, *La crisis política (sus causas y remedios)* (Havana: Imprenta y Papelería "La Universal," 1919); idem, "La decadencia cubana: conferencia de renovación patriótica," *Revista Bimestre Cubana* 47 (January–February 1924): 17–44; Pelayo Pérez, "El peligro amarillo y el peligro negro," *Cuba Contemporánea* 9 (November 1915): 251–259; José Antonio Ramos, *Entreactos* (Havana: R. Veloso Editores, 1913); José Sixto de Sola, "El pesimismo cubano," *Cuba Contemporánea* 3 (December 1913): 273–303; idem, "Los extranjeros en Cuba," *Cuba Contemporánea* 8 (June 1915): 105–128; Carlos M. Trelles, "El progreso y el retroceso de la República de Cuba," *Revista Bimestre Cubana* 18, no. 4 (July–August 1923): 313–319, and 18, no. 5 (September–October 1923): 345–364; Carlos de Velasco, "El problema negro," *Cuba Contemporánea* 1 (February 1913): 73–79; idem, *Aspectos nacionales* (Havana: Jesús Montero, 1915).

53. Figueras, *Cuba y su evolución colonial*, pp. 189–191, 238.

54. Ibid., pp. 147–149.

55. Ibid., p. 152. Figueras does not explain why the Africans, if inferior to the Indians, did not disappear faster.

56. Ibid., pp. 204–205, 251–252.

57. Ibid., p. 208.

58. Ibid., p. 253, also pp. 186–187. The method of calculation is not given by

Figueras.

59. A phenomenon that Figueras also calls "atavism" and *salto atrás* (leap backward): ibid., pp. 240–245.

60. Ibid., p. 440.

61. Ortiz, *La reconquista de América*, pp. 2, 12–26. Like many others, Ortiz noted the example of Japan, which progressed despite the race of its people.

62. Ortiz, *Entre cubanos*, p. 120.

63. Ortiz, *La crisis política*, p. 5.

64. Ortiz, introduction to both *Hampa afrocubana. Los negros brujos* (1st ed., 1906), and *Hampa afrocubana. Los negros esclavos* (1st ed., 1916). See *Los negros esclavos* (Havana: Editorial de Ciencias Sociales, 1975), p. 29.

65. Ortiz, *Los negros esclavos*, pp. 28–29.

66. Ibid., p. 27.

67. Ortiz, *Los negros brujos*, pp. 391, 374.

68. Ibid., p. 401. See also pp. 373–402; and Juan del Morro [Fernando Ortiz], "La Sociedad de Folklore Cubano," *Revista Bimestre Cubana* 18, no. 1 (January–February 1923): 47–52.

69. Hugh Thomas, *Cuba: The Pursuit of Freedom* (New York: Harper & Row, 1971), pp. 432, 517; Pedro Serviat, *El problema negro en Cuba y su solución definitiva* (Havana: Empresa Poligráfica del CC del PCC, 1986), pp. 71–72.

70. Leopoldo Horrego Estuch, *Juan Gualberto Gómez, un gran inconforme* (Havana: Editorial Mecenas, 1949), p. 153; Tomás Fernández Robaina, "El negro en Cuba, 1902–1958. Apuntes para la historia de la lucha contra la discriminación racial en la neocolonia" (unpublished), chap. 3, p. 5.

71. Frederico Chang, *El ejército nacional en la república neocolonial, 1899–1933* (Havana: Editorial de Ciencias Sociales, 1981), pp. 5–10, 137–138.

72. "Ley de inmigración y colonización del 11 de julio de 1906," in República de Cuba. *Colección legislativa.* Vol. 21: *Leyes, decretos y resoluciones de 1° de julio a 31 de diciembre de 1906* (Havana: Impr. y Papelería de Rambla y Bouza, 1911), pp. 222–223.

73. Juan Guiteras, "Patología médica. La fiebre amarilla considerada como enfermedad de la infancia en los focos antillanos," in *La ciencia en Cuba. Recompilación por José Manuel Carbonell y Rivero* (Havana: Imprenta Montalvo y Cárdenas, 1928), p. 225.

74. Juan Guiteras, "Estudios demográficos. Aclimatación de la raza blanca en los trópicos," *Revista Bimestre Cubana* 8, no. 2 (November–December 1913): 413. See also Gustavo Enrique Mustelier, *La extinción del negro. Apuntes político–sociales* (Havana: Impr. de Rambla, Bouza y Ca., 1912), which is much inspired by Ingenieros.

75. For example, "Baturrillo Coincidencias" by Aramburu in *El Diario de la Marina*, 23 April 1910, p. 1; Renée Méndez Capote, *Memorias de una cubanita que nació con el siglo* (1964. Reprint. Habana: Instituto Cubano del Libro, 1976), pp. 20–22, 146–153.

76. "We are not Hottentots, but lucid, free beings, civilized men, who know how much they have done in the time of the martyr and how much they deserve and hope to get now" (Juan F. Risquet, *La cuestión político-social en la isla de Cuba* [Havana: Tipografía "América," 1900], p. 4).

77. For example, Martín Morúa Delgado, "Factores sociales" (1892), in *Obras completas*, 6 vols. (Havana: Edición de la Comisión Nacional del Centenario de Martín Morúa Delgado, 1957), III: 209–237.

78. For example, Juan Gualberto Gómez: See Octavio R. Costa, *Juan Gualberto Gómez, una vida sin sombra* (Havana: Editorial Unidad, 1950), pp. 185–186; and Rosalie Schwartz, "The Displaced and the Disappointed: Cultural Nationalists and Black Activists in Cuba in the 1920s" (PhD diss., University of California, San Diego, 1977), p. 173.

79. Rafael Serra, *Para blancos y negros. Ensayos políticos, sociales y económicos* (Havana: Imprenta "El Score," 1907), p. 92, also pp. 69–79, 91–94. Serra somewhat idealized the achievements of North American blacks and the help of the U.S. government. For a Marxist discussion of his position, see Serviat, *El problema negro*, pp. 75–78.

80. Fernández, "El negro en Cuba," chap. 3, pp. 16–18. Thomas T. Orum, "The Politics of Color: The Racial Dimension of Cuban Politics during the Early Republican Years, 1900–1912," PhD diss., New York University, 1975, pp. 100–201;Louis A. Pérez, Jr., *Cuba under the Platt Amendment, 1902–1934* (Pittsburgh: University of Pittsburgh Press, 1986), pp. 94–103, 150.

81. Sala tercera de lo criminal, Juzgado de instrucción de la sección segunda, Causa #321/1910, Archivo Nacional de Cuba, Fondo de la Audiencia de La Habana, Leg. 529-1, 228-1, 229-1, and 529-4 (esp. Leg. 229-1, 3r rollo, fol. 437–438).

82. Morúa, *Obras completas*, III: 239–245. The amendment was opposed for its unconstitutionality in the Senate and outside, notably by Ortiz (Serafín Portuondo Linares, *Los Independientes de Color. Historia del Partido Independiente de Color* [Havana: Publicaciones del Ministerio de Educación, 1950], pp. 81–104; Ortiz, *Entre cubanos*, pp. 99–101; idem, *Los negros esclavos*, p. 391.

83. Rafael Fermoselle, *Política y color en Cuba. La Guerrita de 1912* (Montevideo: Editorial Geminis, 1974), pp. 102–104, 169–199; Fernández,"El negro en Cuba," chap. 4, pp. 2–4, 7–8, 13–20; Robert B. Hoernel, "Sugar and Social Change in Oriente, Cuba, 1898–1946," *Journal of Latin American Studies* 8, no. 2 (November 1976): 232–233; Louis A. Pérez, Jr., "Politics, Peasants, and People of Color: The 1912 'Race War' in Cuba Reconsidered," *Hispanic American Historical Review* 66, no. 3 (August 1986): 509–539; Portuondo, *Los Independientes*, pp. 197–281; Serviat, *El problema negro*, pp. 80–96. Further research may clarify many aspects of this rebellion.

84. Rafael Conte and José M. Capmany, *Guerra de razas (negros contra blancos en Cuba)* (Havana: Imprenta Militar Antonio Pérez, 1912), pp. 8, 9, 119.

85. Carlos de Velasco, "El problema negro," pp. 73–79.

86. Fernández, "El negro en Cuba," chap. 7, pp. 8–9, chap. 8, pp. 4–12. The

interviews I had with Afro-Cubans in Santiago de Cuba in 1987 tended to indicate that even today the meaning of these events is understood in racial terms: Carlos Nicot (journalist), Enrique Cordiez (pharmacist), and Luciano Hernández (archivist).

87. León Primelles, *Crónica cubana 1915–1918. La reelección de Menocal y la revolución de 1917. La danza de los millones. La primera guerra mundial* (Havana: Editorial Lex, 1955), pp. 111, 221, 537; idem, *Crónica cubana 1919–1922. Menocal y la Liga nacional. Zayas y Crowder. Fin de la danza de los millones y reajuste* (Havana: Editorial Lex, 1957), pp. 134–137, 292, 593; Diego Vicente Tejera, "El hondo problema de la pena de muerte," *Cuba Contemporánea* 42 (September–October 1926): 5–56; idem, "Comentarios al proyecto de código criminal cubano," *Revista Bimestre Cubana* 21, no. 6 (November–December 1926): 846–862; Julio Villoldo, "El lynchamiento, social y jurídicamente considerado," *Cuba Contemporánea* 21 (September 1919): 5–19.

88. José Sixto de Sola, "Los extranjeros en Cuba," pp. 105–128; Carlos de Velasco, "El problema religioso," *Cuba Contemporánea* 8 (July 1915): 209–223.

89. Hoernel, "Sugar and Social Change," pp. 234–235; Pérez, *Cuba 1902–1934*, p. 78; Thomas, *Cuba*, pp. 497–500, 524–525, 540.

90. Pelayo Pérez, "El peligro amarillo y el peligro negro," pp. 257–259; Trelles, "El progreso y el retroceso de la república de Cuba," pp. 351–352.

91. Primelles, *Crónica cubana 1915–1918*, p. 72; idem, *Crónica cubana 1919–1922*, pp. 134, 136, 241; República de Cuba. Secretaría de Estado (Documentos diplomáticos), *Copia de la correspondencia cambiada entre la legación de su Majestad británica en la Habana y la Secretaría de Estado de la República, relativa al trato de los inmigrantes jamaiquinos* (Havana: n.p., 1924), pp. 3–8.

92. Walterio Carbonell, *Crítica. Cómo surgio la cultura nacional* (Havana: Editorial Yaka, 1961), pp. 24–25.

93. For example, "Nuestra Revolución," in *La Vanguardia* (Socialist party newspaper), 25 November 1918.

94. Colette Guillaumin, *L'idéologie raciste. Genèse et langage actuel* (Paris: Mouton, 1972); and Loren R. Graham, "Science and Values: The Eugenics Movement in Germany and Russia in the 1920s," *American Historical Review* 82, no. 5 (December 1977): 1113–1164 have been particularly useful.

95. For example, Ramos Mejía, *Las multitudes argentinas*, inspired by Gustave Le Bon's theories, is padded with scientific metaphors.

4. Racism, Revolution, and *Indigenismo*: Mexico, 1910–1940

ALAN KNIGHT

In this chapter I discuss the part that "race" and racial theories played in revolutionary Mexico, that is, in the Mexico that emerged from the armed revolution of 1910–1920. I have therefore chosen a fairly broad and sweeping approach, sacrificing detail for generalization, in the hope of facilitating cross-cultural comparison. I have also tried to go beyond the written word—the public and published statements of key thinkers—and to relate their statements to their social and historical context. Of course, certain thinkers/writers/politicians were important in enunciating racial theories, particularly in regard to the place of the Indian in revolutionary Mexico: Manuel Gamio and José Vasconcelos, later Alfonso Caso and Gonzalo Aguirre Beltrán.[1] Since they addressed the question directly and publically, their opinions can be readily seized—and, in the middle sections of this chapter, they will be discussed. But an analysis that confines itself to the major thinkers can easily become abstract and rarefied; it may become an armchair quest for intellectual genealogies and relationships whose connection to broader historical trends—social, political, ideological—remains conjectural. How genuinely influential, for example, were Vasconcelos' notion of the "cosmic race" or Molina Enríquez's racial categorization of Mexican society?[2]

Of course, measuring the broad impact of ideas within society is notoriously difficult, especially when, as in this case, the ideas themselves—relating to racial equality or inequality—are embedded deep in social relations, may rarely be overtly expressed, and, indeed, may be deliberately disguised or disingenuously denied. Thus, while the official ideology of revolutionary Mexico has certainly been strenuously resistant to the classic Eurocentric racism, it would be wrong to infer from this that Mexican society is correspondingly free of racist beliefs and practices or that the latter remain, at worst, mere vestigial remnants of a moribund racism.[3] The final section of the chapter will therefore touch on the question of racism in Mexican society, and will attempt to link theory to practice—will try, in other words, to test, in brief and tentative fashion, the impact of the theories previously discussed.

The chapter thus deals not only with racial ideas, their content, logic and provenance, but also with the social impact they achieved. The analysis proceeds from theory to practice, from formal statements to informal relations, from the study to the street. But one further and longer clarification must be made at the outset, for any analysis of Mexican racism demands some grasp of Mexican race relations as they have historically developed. We need some roughly objective guideline against which to set both articulate racial theories and diffuse racial attitudes. Both theories and attitudes, of course, can be of signal importance, for all their subjectivity, prejudice, and even absurdity: "Most of us are aware," Ashley Montagu comments, "that in a very real sense nothing can be more real than the unreal."[4] It is not sufficient, however, simply to recognize the power of racial theories and attitudes, taking this as the only historical given. Such a "phenomenological" approach— whereby "if men typify a situation as racial, racial it must be"—obviously fails to consider the reality beyond perception and, in doing so, makes it harder to understand how perceptions are constructed.[5] I shall therefore start with an analysis of the "reality" of race in Mexico, before proceeding to the more relevant question of theories and attitudes.

The "Reality" of Race

Modern Mexico is a racial mix. This commonplace, the starting point for a host of theories, has no intrinsic explanatory power. The supposed genetic bases of "racial" differentiation have never been proven and, in consequence, the very category "race" has been rightly questioned.[6] The modern Mexican population is, however, a mixture of several groups who displayed contrasting somatic features; in particular, it is the result of Indian and Spanish miscegenation since the sixteenth-century. Other "racial" groups—blacks, in particular—also contributed to this mix, but in this chapter it is the fundamental Indian/Spanish polarity that will be considered.[7]

The colonial regime that prevailed in Mexico (New Spain) for three centuries sought to preserve a degree of separation between Indian and Spaniard: careful "racial"—or castelike—divisions were maintained; power and privilege correlated closely with "racial" identification (an identification that was, of course, cultural as well as biological). In many respects, therefore, colonial Mexico conformed to the model of a caste or "estamental" society, within which ascriptive groups—whites, mestizos, Indians, as well as many subcategories—enjoyed differential access to power and property. Over time, however, such caste or castelike barriers eroded. Miscegenation proceeded apace, bureaucratic impediments notwithstanding. No rigid apartheid could be sustained, and the sheer proliferation of "racial" subtypes attested to the impossibility of thorough categorization.[8] Increasingly—and the change crystallized during the economic boom of the eighteenth century—caste became secondary to class as a form of social identification. By the late eighteenth century "the term 'Indian' ... meant more as a fiscal category than as an ethnic one."[9] With Mexican independence (1821) and the liberal reforms of the mid-nineteenth century came a further demolition of the mechanisms that maintained castelike differentiation. By the time of the Porfirio Díaz regime (1876–1911), all Mexicans stood as formally equal citizens before the law; "racial" labels were still applied by census enumerators but such labels carried no *formal* social or political connotations.

By then, of course, generations of miscegenation had thoroughly blurred the neat "racial" divisions of the early colony. In respect of somatic attributes, few Mexicans were "pure" Indians or whites (*criollos*/creoles); most were mestizos of one sort or another. True, "Indians" were seen to be darker, but "Indians" were not defined solely or even primarily in somatic terms. A range of other characteristics determined "racial"—or, we should properly say, *ethnic*—identification: language, dress, religion, social organization, culture and consciousness. Since these were social rather than innate biological attributes, they were capable of change; the ethnic status of both individuals and communities was not immutable. By dint of education, migration, and occupational shifts (in short, the catchall of "acculturation" or what some prefer to term "de-Indianization") Indians could become mestizos. Individual transitions were possible (with difficulty); collective transitions formed an integral part of the long process of Mexican "development." Upwardly mobile individuals were "whitened": the dictator Díaz ("an almost pure Mixtec" Indian, according to one historian) was, to a contemporary, "of supposed [*sic*] only one-eighth Indian blood" and, in fact, "probably all white."[10] Social mobility thus created an optical illusion, in Mexico as elsewhere in Latin America.[11] More significant were the collective transitions, which can be traced both geographically and chronologically: the pronounced gradient of community acculturation that Redfield discerned running geographically from the (white/mestizo) northwest of the Yucatán peninsula to the (Indian) southeast; the "surprisingly clear-cut gradient of linguistic acculturation" which Friedrich sees chronologically spanning recent generations of Naranjeños.[12] Such patterns of acculturation are sufficiently clear, it seems, for some anthropologists to offer confident timetables of future transformations.[13] Clearly, therefore, the process of *mestizaje*, sometimes seen as basically racial, is in fact social; "mestizo" is an achieved as well as an ascribed status—even though achievement may be difficult and, in the case of communities, may span decades.

The nature of this process, however, gives rise to certain analytical problems that we must initially confront. First, since acculturation represents a highly dynamic process, it becomes difficult to generalize about ethnic relations across time and space. Conventionally, Indian communities may be located at any given time on a rough continuum that stretches from the more thoroughly "Indian" (sometimes "tribal") societies, such as Chiapas' Lacandones, across to the more thoroughly integrated "Indian" peasant society of Central Mexico. Redfield plotted such a continuum within the Yucatán peninsula (from Tusik to Dzitas—and, ultimately, Mérida); Manuel Gamio offered a tripartite division of the continuum, typified by (a) the Maya of Quintana Roo, (b) the Yaquis of Sonora, and (c) the "Indians" of Morelos who had followed Emiliano Zapata's banner in the Revolution.[14] Sometimes, the attribution of "Indian" is reserved for those groups located toward the

"Indian" end of the continuum (the Lacandones, the Quintana Roo Maya, the Yaquis): groups that retain strong linguistic and cultural characteristics, and which are chiefly located in so-called "regions of refuge," where an embattled Indian culture has survived, marginalized though not isolated. Conversely, according to this strict attribution, Central Mexican communities—Catholic, bilingual, suffused with supposedly "Hispanic" culture—are deemed mestizo. Yet, it has been objected, these communities display many of the diagnostic features of Indian society, in terms not only of language but also of social and religious organization. For that reason, some analysts would greatly expand the presumed "Indian" population of Mexico. Thus, while census figures would suggest that around one-third of Mexico's population was "Indian" at the time of the Revolution, Manuel Gamio—chiefly by adding in Central Mexican "Indians," such as those of Morelos—arrived at an estimate of two-thirds.[15] So, too, in specific states: Chiapas was officially reckoned to be 38 percent "Indian" in the 1930s, yet a critic proposed 80 percent as the correct figure. More recently, protagonists of "Indianism" (*sic*) have denounced the "statistical ethnocide," whereby Indian numbers are systematically underestimated.[16]

The problem, of course, is not so much one of statistical accuracy as of ethnic categorizations, which in turn reflect more general sociopolitical assumptions. Different observers—most of them aiming to achieve a neat dichotomy—slice up the broad Indian-mestizo continuum in different ways, using different criteria. Roughly, we can distinguish between official (census-taking) observers, who tend to favor a narrower category of "Indian" (based on language), and unofficial indigenista spokespersons who prefer a broader and thus more numerous "Indian" category. Both positions are, in a sense, political and polemical, and we need subscribe to neither; but we must recognize at the outset the marked discrepancies that occur whenever attempts are made to slice a long continuum into two (or more) discrete parts. And it bears repeating that these slices are socially, not racially, determined; even in respect to inherited somatic features "Indian" and "mestizo" people may be indistinguishable, individually or collectively.[17]

A second problem, highly relevant to the present discussion, concerns the *subjective* nature of Indian/mestizo status. Since it depends on a range of perceived characteristics, rather than on any immutable and innate attributes, status is obviously subjective. There may be broad agreement on Indian status in some cases, but not in others (and these others are far from being a small borderline minority). When perceptions differ in this fashion, whose judgment is to prevail? A key distinction must be made between the intrinsic perception of the individual or community on the one hand, and the extrinsic perception of outside observers—politicians, census-takers, gringo anthropologists—on the other, for the two may not tally. Depending on the criteria used, an individual or community may be deemed Indian or mestizo; an individual may seem a mestizo (or Ladino) to his erstwhile fellow-Indians, but remain an Indian in mestizo eyes.[18] An "Indian" in El Salvador, Marroquín suggests, might pass for a mestizo in Guatemala.[19]

Some commentators, such as Alfonso Caso, lay heavy stress on the subjective perception of the community. A community is Indian if it considers itself Indian, whatever its social and cultural make-up; thus, at the individual level, "an Indian is one who feels that he belongs to an indigenous community," while "a group which lacks the sentiment of being Indian cannot be considered as such."[20] We have here an extreme formulation of the "phenomenological" approach, albeit the burden of definition is transferred from external society to the social actors themselves. Self-definition is, no doubt, a significant criterion, but this seems an excessive and problematic estimate of its importance. Self-definition is hard to get at; it may be fluid and often contradictory; above all, it may—and, in this case, certainly does—depend upon external determinants. A community's self-definition, in other words, may be imposed from outside, in which case the neat criterion of self-definition masks external attributions and prejudices. Indeed, it seems likely that "Indian" identification is indeed imposed from without and, I shall suggest, negatively defined: "a person [in Hueyapan] is more or less Indian in relation to somebody else," hence "Indianness"—rather like "peasantness"—must be conceived in relational terms, with self-definition forming but one part of a much larger complex.[21]

Indians are therefore socially defined, with race being used as a common but genetically unsound shorthand for ethnicity. But, as Montagu put it, unreal—that is, untrue—beliefs can acquire great power. As such, they deserve analysis irrespective of their untruth. The attribution of Indian identity began, of course, with the Conquest: "it was the European who created the Indian."[22] Thereafter, attributions changed, racial theories came and went, doctrines of *indigenismo* were developed. But throughout these were primarily the constructs of non-Indians: "Indian," as a term either of abuse or of praise, was conceived and applied by non-Indians. No common Indian sentiment preceded the Conquest; it was only in the wake of the Conquest that the generic concept of "Indian" could be formulated in negative contradistinction to the dominant Spaniard/European. And this generic concept remained part of Spanish rather than Indian usage. It defined those who were not Spanish or mestizo and it lumped together a wide range of Indian groups, languages, and communities. The Indians themselves lacked any shared sentiment of Indian-ness (pan-Indianism is a very recent creation); they often lacked even the "tribal" allegiances imputed to them, in that they gave their primary loyalty to the community—to the old Mesoamerican *atlepetl,* which the Spaniards had seen fit to conserve (or, with the *congregación,* to replicate) in the interests of social order and economic organization. Thus, a colonial elite confronted what was for it a relatively undifferentiated Indian mass; while—in terms of subjective consciousness—the Indian mass was divided into myriad semiautonomous communities, often mutually hostile and, certainly in populous Central Mexico, lacking any coherent tribal allegiance. Colonial government—and colonial Indian rebellions—reflected this atomistic pattern.[23]

The colony "created" the Indian in one further respect. The blending of Spanish and Indian cultures, paralleling the blending of Spanish and Indian blood, ensured that many of the features that were later taken to be "Indian" were in fact of European origin (just as some "European" traits were of Indian origin). Thus, "Indian" food, dress, technology, religion, and social organization—the whole battery of social traits diagnostic of the Indian—were all infused with Spanish elements: the "pure" Indian was as rare culturally as biologically. When later *indigenistas* set out to recover a pristine Indian culture, they either attempted the impossible or, more realistically, they took the syncretic culture of the colonial Indian as their yardstick. Precisely because this was a syncretic culture—a fusion of earlier cultures into one that was new and different—it becomes somewhat pointless to produce checklists of pristine Indian as against imported Spanish/mestizo elements or to try to sort them into piles of positive Indian assets and negative colonial accretions.[24]

Neither independence nor the Porfiriato changed this colonial pattern of unequal reciprocal definition. Of course, the formal status of the Indians changed; protective colonial legislation (already waning during the eighteenth century) lapsed; economic development further eroded community resources; and, by the later nineteenth century, Porfirian state-building curbed communal political autonomy. Nevertheless, on the eve of the Revolution, there was scant evidence of a broad "Indian" consciousness (comparable to the nascent "peasant" consciousness that some historians have discerned in this period). Linguistic differences remained, rival communities still feuded incessantly, primary allegiances were given to the community (and/or to the cacique, or boss) rather than to any supra-communal entity.

Hence, the Revolution that began in 1910 could be fought and was fought on the basis of considerable Indian participation (more so if the broad definition of "Indian" is adopted), but in the absence of any self-consciously Indian project. True, there were abundant *agrarian* demands/programs/projects—some local, some regional, some national; and these were not, as sometimes suggested, primarily the work of manipulative leaders and intellectuals; they reflected genuine popular—including Indian—grievances. But they were usually couched in class rather than caste terms; they pitted peasants against landlords, not Indians against whites or mestizos. Incidents of ethnic conflict occurred—Zapatistas disliked city slickers, the Naranjeños' attacked mestizo interlopers—but these were manifestations of agrarian (i.e., class) polarization and did not form part of a sustained policy of *Indian* self-assertion (indeed, the "Indian" label, I shall note, was used as a deliberate smear by opponents).[25]

The chief exception was the Yaqui Indian rebellion in the northwest, which fused peasant and Indian struggles in a sustained resistance to *yori* (white/mestizo) exploitation. But the Yaqui rebellion was precisely an exception. In Southern Mexico, where Indian populations (even narrowly defined) remained numerous, agrarian revolt was weak, and Indian participation in the Revolution tended to depend on the leadership of local caciques, committed to the defense of regional autonomy: in the Sierra Juárez of Oaxaca, for example, or the highlands of Chiapas.

Thus, where attributions of *Indian* rebellion cropped up, they were more often polemical attacks by hostile—and fearful—outsiders than proud statements of Indian rebels themselves. When Tuxtla Gutiérrez warred with San Cristóbal for supremacy in Chiapas, the *tuxtlecos* made free with allegations of caste war alleging their opponents were "Indians." Zapatismo, it is important to note, was linked to the "Indian" cause first by outraged planters, who similarly shrilled the dangers of caste war, and later by *indigenista* reformers like Gamio (and even Vasconcelos), who chose to see Zapatismo, in retrospect, as the awakening of the Indian people of Morelos.[26]

This *indigenista* appropriation—and misattribution—was necessary precisely because the Indian contribution to the Revolution had been so anonymous. Plenty of Indians had fought, but not *qua* Indians (the same could be said, for example, of Catholics, or even of women). The conscious *indigenismo* that came to permeate official circles after the armed Revolution was not, therefore, the product of direct Indian pressure (one could contrast the agrarian reform which *was* to a significant degree the result of *agrarista* pressure). Perhaps for that very reason it could be safely adopted: *indigenismo* came more easily to Mexican elites than, say, to Andean elites, for whom the threat of caste war and reversion to barbarism seemed truly present.[27] *Indigenistas* like Gamio therefore had to display a certain ingenuity in order to justify their position: "it is not the Indian who made the Revolution," he conceded, "nevertheless, its deepest roots grew and continue to grow in the Indian race." Or again: "the revolutionary movements never took shape or rose up in the heart [of the Indian population], yet it was in that population that it found its primordial origin."[28]

Postrevolutionary *indigenismo* thus represented yet another non-Indian formulation of the "Indian problem"; it was another white/mestizo construct (specifically, Aguirre Beltrán stresses, a mestizo one), part of a long tradition stretching back to the Conquest.[29] Certainly it was a more enlightened and sympathetic formulation than its colonial or Porfirian predecessors. But, like them, it involved the imposition of ideas, categories, and policies from outside. The Indians themselves were the objects, not the authors, of indigenismo. This the *indigenistas* frankly admitted. As Gamio apostrophized this "poor and suffering race:" "you will not awaken spontaneously. It will be necessary for friendly hearts to work for your redemption." The "intellectual baggage of the Indian race," Gamio went on, weighed them down, retarding consciousness and action. The Indian suffers, "but unfortunately does not understand, does not know, the appropriate means to achieve his liberation." It was therefore the task of skilled and sympathetic intellectuals, ethnographers, and anthropologists above all, to "forge . . . an Indian soul."[30]

If, in this respect, revolutionary *indigenismo* was simply the latest in a long line of elite formulations of the "Indian problem"; it acquired a distinctive significance because it coincided with the social upheaval of the Revolution (roughly, 1910–1920). This brings me to the empirical crux of this chapter: the connections linking the Revolution to racial ideas and relations. Many such connections have been asserted, then and since; in discussing them, we must guard against the perennial danger of attributing all post-1910 change to the thaumaturgic power of the Revolution (and thus neglecting common global trends that may have influenced Mexican thought and practice). A careful analysis must start with some sort of perspective. What was the status of racial ideas and relations on the eve of the Revolution? How did they change and why?

The Impact of Revolution

We have noted that the nineteenth century saw a progressive breakdown of the castelike, colonial order and its replacement by a society stratified by class. Van den Berghe, who takes Mexico as one of his key cases, sees a "paternalist" colonial model giving way to class-based society in which "racial" divisions (that is, ethnic divisions that are often deemed racial) lost their social significance. But this is too sweeping. Independent Mexico did not go the way of a *Herrenvolk* society, but neither did it eliminate ethnic in favor of class stratification. As in the colony, the two coexisted and, while the balance gradually tipped from caste to class, this was a long, slow process, still far from complete at the time of the Revolution.[31] Class now counted for more, but caste—ethnic status—was far from irrelevant. Indians were usually peasants, but they were not peasants *tout court*, as some on the Left have chosen to argue. Rather, they were peasants who suffered a double oppression: "as poor peasants, resident peons, and city lumpenproletariat, they suffered an exploitation characteristic of their social class position; and, as ethnic groups in a condition of inferiority vis-à-vis mestizos and creoles, they were culturally oppressed by the carriers of the dominant culture, that is, they suffered an exploitation characteristic of their colonial situation."[32]

What is more, it seems probable that racism, buttressed by racial theories, became stronger in the course of the nineteenth century. The question cannot be fully discussed here. However, powerful ideological as well as economic factors favored the development of a more virulent racism in the later nineteenth century. The heyday of European racist thought—dated from approximately 1850 to 1920—roughly coincided with Mexico's phase of liberal state-building and capitalist export-oriented economic development. Both of these processes, which culminated in the neo-liberal or "order and progress" dictatorship of Porfirio Díaz (1876–1911), lent themselves to racist interpretations and rationalizations. At the intellectual level, Porfirian thinkers were profoundly influenced by social Darwinism; Spencer's evolutionism, with its denigration of human hybrids, exercised a strong appeal.[33] Policymakers, convinced of the superiority of the white European, vainly sought to attract immigrants to Mexico: they were needed, as Justo Sierra explained, "so as to obtain a cross with the indigenous race, for only European blood can keep the level of civilization . . . from sinking, which would mean regression, not evolution."[34]

Yet more significant and pervasive, I would suggest, was the inherent logic of the

Porfirian model of development, which required the dispossession of peasant communities (many of them Indian) and the creation of a reliable labor force, urban and rural. These trends were not new; they followed old colonial precedents. But the pressures and opportunities were now far greater (not least thanks to the advent of the railway) and they lent themselves to new racist and social Darwinist rationalizations. As in colonial countries, the "myth of the lazy native" was invoked—by foreign and Mexican employers—to explain peasant resistance to proletarianization and to justify tough measures to overcome it.[35] The coffee planters of Chiapas deplored the "natural indolence" of the sierra Indians; a Morelos planter lamented that "the Indian . . . has many defects as a laborer, being, as he is, lazy, sottish and thieving."[36] Only by strict discipline, which in Yucatán and elsewhere became virtual slave-driving, could these traits be countered.[37]

Meanwhile, the Porfirian elite was also engaged in the parallel task of state-building. Here, the Indian figured as an antinational element requiring prompt and, if necessary, forcible assimilation. Some Porfirian thinkers, foreshadowing postrevolutionary *indigenismo*, looked to the transforming power of education.[38] In this respect, we can detect clear continuities stretching from Porfiriato to Revolution, and we can rightly question the old *leyenda negra* of undiluted Porfirian racism.[39] In practice, however, Porfirian *indigenismo* was more rhetorical than real: its material manifestations were statues of Cuauhtémoc in Mexico City rather than Indian schools in the countryside.[40] Even when rural schools were established, the teachers who went among the Indians were quite capable of displaying racist hauteur.[41] In this respect, Porfirian *indigenismo* belonged to an old tradition of elite indigenismo, which appealed to Creole nationalist sentiment, but which implied no genuine social reform, no real amelioration of Indian life.[42]

Furthermore, irrespective of shifts in elite intellectual fashion, the practice of the Porfirian regime was one of Indian oppression. If the regime offered its subjects the famous *pan o palo* ("bread or the club") alternative, it was the second half of the formula that Indian populations came to know and fear. Individual communities suffered agrarian dispossession, and collective groups, which had maintained a degree of "tribal" independence, were forcibly integrated: in Yucatán, where the rebel Maya were finally defeated, and in Sonora, where the old Yaqui war reached a new crescendo. These large-scale Indian wars—integral parts of the Porfirian state-building project—were carried out with all the operational and ideological panoply of U.S. or Argentine frontier expansion. In Sonora, the Yaquis were hunted down, deported, and enslaved; genocide was justified by the Yaquis' stubborn refusal to submit to the rule of the nation-state.[43] In the final years of the Porfiriato (no emergent *indigenismo* here) the campaign became a virtual crusade, carried through with fanatical disregard for its deleterious economic consequences, as a racist ideology triumphed over the self-interest even of the landlord class.[44] The parallel with formal colonialism, evident in the economic domain, was thus repeated in the political and ideological. Not only were the natives lazy, they were also stubbornly refractory to civilized rule. Quasi-colonial attitudes and methods became hallmarks of the Porfiriato: the army resembled a colonial force (pale officers, dark troops) and resorted to the usual counterinsurgency excesses; state governors displayed a proconsular disdain for their subject populations.[45] The logic of Porfirian "development" thus conspired with imported ideology to create a climate of racism that was both official (that is, justified, albeit not uniformly, by elite intellectuals) and, more important, unofficial (practiced by the regime's minions and by social elites more generally).

It is against this backdrop that the Revolution must be set. How did the Revolution affect this prevalent racism? It is sometimes said that it brought emphatic change, that the elimination of racism and the rehabilitation of the Indian were central, even *the* central, elements within the revolutionary project: "In some sense it can be said that the very essence of the Revolution is based upon the vindication of the Indian and of the Indian community."[46] Certainly a change can be discerned in the realm of official rhetoric—a realm more vulnerable to ideological coups and upheavals than the torpid kingdom of custom and prejudice. The new regime, raising the standard of the 1917 Constitution and consolidating itself through the 1920s, incorporated *indigenismo* into its official ideology.[47] It claimed, in other words, to seek the emancipation and integration of Mexico's exploited Indian groups: emancipation from the old oppressions of landlord, cacique, and *cura* (priest); integration into the new revolutionary state and nation.

Integration was not, of course, a new objective or accomplishment. But in the past, the revolutionary *indigenistas* argued, it had been achieved by means of coercion and at the expense of the Indians' pre-existent culture. Now, in contrast, integration would be planned, enlightened, and respectful of that culture: Indian economic and intellectual development could proceed, Gamio argued, "without this, of course, signifying the annihilation of the original [Indian] culture." At the interface of ethnic contact and acculturation Indian-fighting generals would give way to applied anthropologists; meanwhile, Indian culture would receive due respect, Indian history would be rehabilitated.[48] Accordingly, the more enlightened (or optimistic?) *indigenistas* believed that integration could proceed without de-Indianization; indeed, an Indian population genuinely integrated—that is, educated, bilingual, and politically mobilized—could better sustain its own culture (language, dress, religion, mores) than one that remained marginalized, uneducated, monolingual, and politically inert.[49]

Constituting, as it did, an official orthodoxy, revolutionary *indigenismo* included a range of emphases and positions. But its varied protagonists shared a common belief in the need to integrate the Indian, albeit in an enlightened, noncoercive fashion. Before analyzing this belief, we should note that several alternative positions existed. The old policy of coercive integration, which, I have suggested, represented Porfirian practice, if not entirely Porfirian theory, has been termed by Aguirre Beltrán "rightist Westernism," marked by "excessive esteem for European and Anglo-Saxon culture," "openly racist" attitudes and solutions, and forced acculturation.[50] As an official ideology, this was bankrupt after 1910; as a matter of daily practice it lived on lustily, as I will note. Meanwhile, in opposition to the mainstream *indigenista* current, two further heresies were evident. One—Aguirre Beltrán's "leftist Westernism"—has already been mentioned: It is the belief that Indians are merely peasants, suffering the common oppression of peasants, there-fore deserving no special discriminatory treatment: "The vindication of the Indian fits into the general framework of the economic liberation of the proletarian masses." But, Aguirre Beltrán further notes, this position *in practice* stood pretty close to revolutionary *indigenismo*; in certain cases, like that of President Lázaro Cárdenas, reformers tended to oscillate between the two.[51]

Then, there existed a more radical alternative—Aguirre Beltrán's "Indianism," quite distinct from *indigenismo*—which denied the very imperative of integration, and which asserted the Indians' potential for autonomous development. Indianism could take several forms. Sometimes, it was typified by a vicarious romanticization of Indian history and culture, usually on the part of urban middle class mestizos: parlor Aztecófilos, "erudite contemporary idolaters," as Octavio Paz has called them, people straight from the pages of Lawrence's *Plumed Serpent*.[52] Such "cultural extremists" cultivated a somewhat spurious Indianism and allegedly sought "to rid Mexico of all Spanish and other foreign influences and to revive indigenous traditions"; though their influence and numbers were scant, they could prove vocal, as they showed in the famous furor over the bones of Cuauhtémoc.[53] Other Indianists have argued, more coherently if not always more soberly, for the autonomous development—as against the integration—of the Indian. In the 1930s certain radicals, impressed by the supposed achievements of Soviet policy toward the nationalities, expounded the view that Mexico's Indian groups were, in fact, submerged nationalities, deserving of "national autonomy."[54] More recently, the standard *indigenista*/integrationist position has also been attacked by anthropolo-gists who similarly cite examples of allegedly successful multiethnic nation-building.[55] Finally, in recent years, a vigorous Indianist movement has developed in Mexico and elsewhere in Latin America that roundly rejects the "false states" created at the expense of Indian autonomy, conceives of Indian populations as "potential nations," and—joining hands with the "cultural extremists"—sees In-dian culture (allegedly the only "authentic" culture in the continent) as "a valid alternative in the face of Western civilization."[56]

Though these alternative positions must be noted, it is the mainstream integrationist/ *indigenista* current that deserves chief attention. From the 1910s to the present its representatives have adhered to the principle of enlightened, planned, noncoercive integration and strongly repudiated Indianist heresies. Luis Cabrera, for example, dismissed the "artistic snobbism" of those who sought to revive "Indian customs" and insisted that "the essential problem in regard to the ethnic question consists of achieving homogeneity"; years later, the mainstream *indigenista* spokeman Al-fonso Caso denounced the "raving Indianists" (*indigenistas delirantes*) who, for example, urged "that we should abandon Spanish and speak Nahuatl."[57]

Mainstream indigenismo, advocating the progressive, persuasive integration of the Indian into Mexican society, looked to a range of policies that might advance this objective. Education was the chief weapon in the *indigenista* armory, although, as Gamio stressed, it could not be the only one.[58] Rural and Indian schools were established through the 1920s and 1930s, one of their principal tasks being the training of a new generation of bilingual Indian teachers. The rural school, however, became a center not only of education (neutrally defined), but also of technological diffusion, agrarian reform, political mobilization, and nationalist propaganda. The *maestro rural,* acting, like his French Republican counterpart, as the front-line soldier of the secular state, was expected to counter the influence of the church and to stimulate sentiments of patriotism, to inculcate, as one study puts it, "the new 'religion' of the country—post-Revolutionary nationalism."[59] "Indian" customs, music, dance, and rituals were rehabilitated and woven into a new tapestry of folkloric nationalism; revolutionary martyrs, like Zapata, were claimed for the *indigenista* cause; and reformers like Carrillo Puerto in Yucatán subtly blended radical discourse with traditional Maya symbols.[60] The ejido, the village land grant sanctioned by the agrarian reform program, was somewhat misleadingly equated with the old Aztec *calpullalli*; and a new school of government-backed applied anthropologists—the great champions of *indigenismo* like Gamio and Caso—advanced the study of both contemporary Indian communities and their ancient native American predecessors (the didactic value of historical study was repeatedly emphasized). The most celebrated representatives of this new official philosophy were, of course, the revolutionary muralists, who provided pictorial affirmation of Indian valor, nobility, suffering, and achievement, which they set against a revived black legend of Spanish oppression.

Most authorities agree that the Revolution thus wrought a significant transformation in *official* thinking concerning race and ethnic relations. The old Porfirian racist orthodoxy—an orthodoxy, to be sure, that was neither uniform nor unchallenged—gave way to a new, self-consciously reactive, antiracist orthodoxy. The relative success of this transformation, however, gave rise to the erroneous conclusion that, as if by official fiat, racism had been banished from the land. "Fortunately," Cabrera wrote, "race prejudices do not exist in Mexico," a sentiment echoed later by Caso, as well as by outside observers like Van den Berghe.[61] To state, as I shall in conclusion, that this is a misleading view is neither original nor surprising. However, before reaching that conclusion, it is worth probing somewhat further the character of official revolutionary *indigenismo*; for it could be suggested that its very failure to banish racism from Mexican society is related to its own internal tensions and anomalies.

We should first consider why *indigenismo* flowered as an official philosophy when it did. As an elitist, non-Indian construct, it cannot be attributed to any direct Indian pressure or lobbying; in this, it resembled anticlericalism or economic nationalism (comparable elite "projects") rather than agrarianism (which enjoyed genuine popular roots and, indeed, encountered strenuous elite resistance). First, to guard against the *post hoc ergo propter hoc* fallacy (whereby everything is attributed to the Revolution), we should note a broader Latin American shift toward *indigenismo*, characteristic of the early twentieth century and partly related to the combined cerebral introspection and patriotic junketing of the independence centennial of 1910.[62] Just as economic nationalism was a Latin American trend in which Mexico participated (and would have done so, *mutatis mutandis*, revolution or no), so some form of *indigenismo*—rhetorical, folkloric, nationalist—was on the agenda. As Stabb, Powell, and others have shown, Porfirian thinkers were already reformulating the "Indian problem" well before the Revolution began.[63]

But the Revolution certainly gave a great stimulus to this ideological shift. The Indian contribution to the Revolution had not been premised on any Indianist project but it had revealed the "Indian problem" and brought non-Indians into contact with Indians on a grand scale. (The Chaco War, obviously, had nothing to do with *indigenismo*, but it similarly served to awaken Bolivia's non-Indian intellectuals and *políticos* to "the Indian.") During the Revolution, mestizo commanders like Alvaro Obregón or Gabriel Gavira commanded and depended upon their Indian veterans, Yaquis and Juchitecos, respectively; northern proconsuls like Salvador Alvarado and Jesús Agustín Castro, sent to govern the benighted south, waxed indignant at the degradation and oppression of the Maya. Their sentiments were by no means pure and altruistic, however. Some northerners regarded their southern, Indian compatriots with outright racist contempt; but the proconsuls, governing in distant states, needed to win support against hostile local elites, especially the planter class.[64] *Indigenismo* offered a means to delegitimize these elites, to prize the Indians away from their lamentable deference, and to bind them to the new revolutionary state.[65] In Chiapas, in fact, *indigenismo* eventually emerged as a key weapon in the central government's struggle against local particularism.[66]

The revolutionaries' discovery of the Indian—of the Indian's capacity for either troublesome sedition or supportive mobilization—was paralleled by their commitment to state and nation-building. In both respects, of course, they followed Porfirian precedents, but they did not like to admit as much and, like any incoming revolutionary regime, they preferred to distance themselves from their blackguard predecessors. If the Porfiristas had labored to build state and nation, the revolutionaries had to continue the work but to a different tune. The very continuity of practice demanded some abrupt changes of rhetoric. In 1926 the revolutionaries quelled the last Yaqui revolt with an efficiency Don Porfirio would have envied (and it was a revolutionary, Manuel Diéguez, veteran of the famous Cananea strike, who in 1915 coined the inevitable plagiarism: "the only good Yaqui is a dead Yaqui"), but such unfortunate parallels made it all the more necessary to put rhetorical distance between the "revolutionary" present and the "reactionary" past.[67]

This effort involved, first, a commitment to state interference in the realm of ethnic relations. A standard feature of revolutionary ideology was the insistence on the state's role as a social arbiter. The state had a vital, interventionist role, that would enable it to correct major social imbalances and inequalities. This did not mean engineering outright equality but, rather, protecting the weak against the strong in the interests of social equilibrium (another key revolutionary concept). Thus, the state should bolster the infant labor movement in its confrontation with capital—not because capital was inherently malign, but because it was excessively powerful.[68] So, too, the *indigenistas* argued, in so many words, for positive discrimination, which would protect the weak unorganized Indian population. Formal equality before the law, the old liberal nostrum, was meaningless so long as the Indians were denied education, political access, and economic development.[69] The night watchman state had to give way to the *estado papá*, the paternalist state. This shift, of course, responded to state self-interest as well as to considerations of social justice, but it nevertheless involved a repudiation of the strict social Darwinism of the Porfiriato.

Even more important, the Revolution gave a fresh stimulus to the process of nation-building. This process was far from new: the mid-nineteenth-century Reforma has been depicted as an exercise in "liberal nation-building"; Porfirian ideologues—Justo Sierra especially—continued the tradition.[70] But the revolutionaries faced special circumstances. Between 1910 and 1920 the chaos of civil war had shattered the state and reduced Mexico to a patchwork of warring factions. Yucatán and Oaxaca had virtually seceded from the federation. Freelance caudillos, like Peláez in the Huasteca or Cantú in Baja California, ruled in defiance of the central government. Twice the United States had violated Mexico's territory. The task of creating a viable, coherent nation—a nation that was more than a mere "geographical expression"—was never more daunting, never more pressing. It is only in terms of these circumstances that we can understand Carranza's prickly nationalism or Calles' fervid anticlericalism. As for Mexico's Indians, they constituted a major challenge to the nationalist project. For them the nation-state was, at best, a source of fiscal and other demands; they owed it no loyalty (revolutionaries lamented the Indians' blind support of antinational reactionary caudillos like Meixueiro in Oaxaca or Fernández Ruiz in Chiapas); Mexico's Indians lacked "the essential sentiment of the citizen, that political solidarity which is the very base on which the principle of nationality rests."[71] It was vital to inculcate that sentiment, to convert passive subjects into active citizens.

Amid all the rhetoric, exhortation and self-examination that followed the Revolution, one constant theme stands out: that of "forjando patria," in the words of Gamio's celebrated tract.[72] Nationalists like Gamio were explicit about their commitment to create a new nationalism, to combine Mexico's disparate population in a solid patriotic union. There could be no question of creating Indian enclaves or nations: the old liberal horror of *republiquetas de indios* was resurrected in Obregón's denial of Yaqui tribal pretensions, or in Alfonso Caso's later repudiation of a policy of reservations.[73] However, Indian values, myth, and history had a necessary place in the new nationalism. It was not a question of disparaging Mexico's European heritage (as the *outré* Indianists would later do) but rather of recognizing the process of cultural (often called "racial") mixing that had created the unique Mexican people. For, according to the emerging orthodoxy of the

Revolution, the old Indian/European thesis/antithesis had now given rise to a higher synthesis, the mestizo, who was neither Indian nor European, but quintessentially Mexican.

The cult of the mestizo, like so much revolutionary ideology, was not new. It had been hinted at a century earlier by Fray Servando. Justo Sierra (so often a bridge between Porfirian and revolutionary thought) had "defined the mestizo as the dynamic element within the Mexican population," which had risen to power with the Reforma and whose epitome was Porfirio Díaz.[74] But it was with the Revolution that the mestizo cult blossomed. "In the great forge of America," Gamio began his famous work, "on the giant anvil of the Andes, virile races of bronze and iron have struggled for centuries"; from this struggle emerged the mestizo, the "national race" of Mexico, the carrier of "the national culture of the future." Now (1916) it was time for Mexico's rulers "to take up the hammer and gird themselves with the black-smith's apron, so that they may make rise from the miraculous anvil the new nation [*patria*] of blended bronze and iron."[75]

In this formulation, Gamio followed Andrés Molina Enríquez, whose *Grandes problemas nacionales* (1909) had offered a diagnosis of Mexico's ills, based on a mixture of Comte, Spencer, Darwin, and Haeckel. Molina Enríquez analyzed Mexican society in terms of ethnic groups and came close to equating them with social classes.[76] But he stressed, above all, the historic rise of the mestizo, who was destined to dominate Mexico: "The fundamental and unavoidable basis of all the work that in future will be undertaken for the good of the country must be the continuation of the mestizos as the dominant ethnic element and as the controlling political base of the population." Thereby, Mexico could achieve demographic growth without recourse to immigration; the population could become a "national-ity"; and that nationality could "establish with precision its own concept of patriotism."[77] Again, therefore, *mestizaje* and nationhood were equated. Almost thirty years later, Molina Enríquez still harped on this theme, although he had converted his earlier tripartite ethnic scheme into a simple dichotomy in which a minority (15 percent) upper caste [*sic*] of creoles, Spaniards, and "creole/mestizos" confronted an exploited majority (85 percent) lower caste, "that of color, of Indian blood . . . chiefly represented by Indians and Indian/mestizos." He also echoed Gamio's opening motif: "Over time, the anvil of Indian blood will always prevail over the hammer of Spanish blood."[78]

Thus, by the mid-1930s—years of radical *indigenismo*—Molina Enríquez's cult mestizo had been assimilated to the Indian (this mestizo was, we may say, a lopsided rather than a balanced synthesis). But the basic racial schema remained intact, just as the Indian/mestizo remained, for Molina, the essence of Mexican nationality. Molina Enríquez is generally regarded as an important influence on revolutionary thinking. Certainly Luis Cabrera believed as much and echoed some of his conclusions. Mexico's "unification," he argued, "must be achieved around the mestizo element, which is the most numerous and homogeneous element"; thus, the necessary consequence of nation-building was "to dissolve the Indian element in the mestizo element."[79] Lesser ideologues concurred, as did foreign observers like John Lind, Woodrow Wilson's Mexican emissary of 1913–1914 (and their endorsement of mestizo destiny did not go unnoticed).[80]

But the most celebrated cultist of *mestizaje* was, of course, José Vasconcelos, writer, philosopher, and politician, who provided brief but dynamic leadership for the new Ministry of Education from 1921 to 1924. Vasconcelos formulated the idea of the "cosmic race," the new mixed race that would prevail not only in Mexico but in the world at large. Reversing older biological assumptions—those of Spencer and Agassiz, which had deemed hybrids inferior to pure races—Vasconcelos both saw and applauded the process of global mestization. The mestizo was the "bridge to the future"; he also displayed a distinctive character (not entirely dissimilar to Vasconcelos' own self-image): quick, vivacious, subtle, mercurial, lacking prejudice, and loving novelty.[81]

The mestizo thus became the ideological symbol of the new regime. *Indigenismo* fitted well within this vision, since the very aim of the *indigenistas* was, we have seen, to integrate the Indians, in other words to "mestizo-ize" them. Or, rather, as the more thoughtful *indigenistas* put it, the aim was to mestizo-ize the Indians and, at the same time, to Indianize the mestizos, to create a national synthesis on the basis of reciprocal contributions.[82] For the new revolutionary elite, this was a particularly appealing philosophy. First, it was nationalist, mobilizing and agglutinative, appropriate to the political tasks they faced. Second, it fitted their own self-image (not just Vasconcelos'). Were not the victorious northern revolutionaries—as Gamio put it—an "element of mixed blood," an "intermediate race," who now joined hands with their revolutionary allies, the "Indian race" of Central Mexico?[83] Third, the cult of *mestizaje* offered a means to distance revolutionary rhetoric from that of the past, and to do so without falling into the trammels of socialism or communism. Despite certain embarrassing parallels (such as the repression of the Yaquis), and despite the ideological antecedents to be found among Porfirian thinkers, the cult of the mestizo did represent a departure from the cosmopolitan, Europhile ethos of the Porfiriato. The mestizo class could thus be depicted as "the eternal rebel, the traditional enemy of the class of pure blood or foreign blood, the author and director of uprisings and rebellions, and the class which has best understood the just laments of the Indian class."[84]

The new *indigenista-mestizaje* cult thus fitted very comfortably within revolutionary thought. If it was intellectually derivative and unoriginal, it nevertheless acquired unprecedented power and relevance by virtue of the "revolutionary" circumstances of post-1910. It was an idea whose time had come. It is worth pausing to reiterate three key aspects of this new, officially dominant idea. First, it was an idea imposed on the Indian from outside. Second, it embodied the optimistic belief that acculturation could proceed in a guided, enlightened fashion, such that the positive aspects of Indian culture could be preserved, the negative expunged. This belief was optimistic in several respects: it presupposed that the process could be rationally controlled (not least, by applied anthropologists); it tended to perpetuate the notion of a bipartite Indian culture, possessing distinctive and potentially separable Indian and European elements (whereas it would be truer to talk of a tight unitary fusion); and it thus assumed that the adding or subtracting of elements was feasible, if not straightforward. Yet, as more thoughtful students have pointed out, cultures cannot be modified according to simple arithmetical principles of addition and subtraction; cultures are more than the sums of their constituent parts, and those parts cohere in mutual interdependence—and, of course, tension.[85]Elements cannot be removed or added at will; nor, of course, can there be easy agreement as to which elements are desirable, which detrimental.[86]

Third, and most important, *indigenismo* tended to reproduce many of the racist assumptions of the preceding "Westernism," which it formally opposed. It did so because, even where it reacted against Porfirian racism, it continued to operate within the racist paradigm—it could not, in other words, break out of that paradigm, but chose rather to criticize and invert several of its basic tenets. Like Marx, shackled to Ricardian political economy, the *indigenistas* could shake the bars of their conceptual prison but not escape from it. Thus, while some later *indigenistas* exorcised "race" from their schema, insisting that "race'"was, in fact, purely a socially defined category, many others—especially the pioneers—retained "race" as an independent (innate, biological) factor, which operated alongside distinct social and historical factors.

Though their formulation of "race" was not always coherent and explicit, they seemed to argue three positions. Virtually all agreed that racial, that is, innate and probably biologically determined differences were significant, but the earlier "Westernist" assumptions of Indian or mestizo inferiority were wrong. First, for some *indigenistas*, who came to espouse the extreme "Indianist" position mentioned earlier, the Indian or mestizo was actually *superior* to the white. This was straightforward reverse racism. Others, in contrast, argued for innate racial *differences*, but not for racial subordination or superordination. In other words, they saw Indians and whites as innately different, possessing contrasting skills, virtues, and vices, but they did not believe that these differences justified imputations of superiority and inferiority. However, inasmuch as they regarded innate racial differences as significant, they too subscribed to a racist explanation of society. Finally, the mildest—and also the wooliest—view avoided any such explicit assertion of racial difference, but continued to talk of "race" as if it were a meaningful category. Indians were not inferior, nor were they innately distinct from whites, yet they belonged to an Indian "race" and this was a significant fact. Logically, these theorists could have dropped the use of "race" altogether or at least they could have made clear that for them "race" denoted a social category. Instead, they remained prisoners of the preceding racist discourse, and continued to scatter references to "race" among their ostensibly antiracist *indigenista* writings. Inasmuch as politicians, officials, and the public generally tended to follow suit, it can be suggested that the perpetuation of this discourse probably helped maintain both the notion of "race" and, to some degree, the practice of racism.

This perpetuation of racist ideas among a group of thinkers committed to resist the older, Eurocentric racism is hardly surprising. On the one hand, they had in many cases been nurtured in the old tradition—that of Spencerian positivism and social Darwinism. They might react against its Eurocentric conclusions, but they could not entirely free themselves from its pervasive racial categorizations: as Marvin Harris points out, "no major figure in the social sciences between 1860 and 1890 escaped the influence of evolutionary racism."[87] Furthermore, to the extent that racist terminology and assumptions peppered the political discourse of postrevolutionary Mexico, Mexico was not so different from many countries, whose political elites habitually resorted to racist shorthand by way of social explanation well into the twentieth century.[88] And, even when Mexican *indigenistas* strove hardest to expunge Porfirian racism, they easily fell into the familiar error of reverse racism, attributing an innate superiority to the previously "inferior" Indian or mestizo. This was, perhaps, intellectually tempting and even politically shrewd, but it further muddied the waters, perpetuating racial explanations and attribution instead of eliminating them.[89]

Examples are legion. Manuel Gamio strenuously advocated the elevation of the Indian, whose "aptitudes for progress" were the equal of the white's, yet he retained "race" as a crucial independent variable in his social and historical analysis (that is, he did not reduce "race" to ethnicity, a socially and culturally defined identity). Man, he reiterated, is a product of race, language, and culture (Molina Enríquez would have agreed); his character is decisively formed by "the physical-biological-social environment." Mexican history demands a racial explanation. Initially, an "invading race," the "white race," confronted the indigenous "race," of which some "Indians of pure blood" still remained. The Reforma favored the "mixed race" (shades of Sierra) but, as in Latin America generally, Mexico failed to create a genuine, unitary nation—after the model of France, Germany, or Japan, nations from which "there arises a solemn cry of shared blood, of shared flesh, that cry which is above all else, since it is the voice of life, the mysterious force which pulls material together and resists its disintegration." Only in Yucatán, Gamio suggested, had a comparable fusion resulted: only Yucatán displayed "that racial homogeneity, that unification of physical types, that advanced, happy fusion of races [which] constitutes the first and most solid basis of nationalism" (and this homogeneity is physically demonstrable in the predominant brachycephalism of the peninsula's population). It is the task of the Revolution—itself the work of "two social classes, two races"—to replicate that outcome nationwide.[90]

Although such views place Gamio in category three—*indigenista* protagonists of racial equality and national unification who, superfluously and perhaps danger-ously, perpetuated explanatory notions of race—he also occasionally slips into category two, arguing for racial *differences* (but not racial *inferiorities/superiori-ties*). The Indian's capacity for work and privation, for example, exceeds that of the white, though the latter may display more power on the job. Of Mexico's Indians he comments: "We will not find, save in very few countries, human entities whose

President Lázaro Cárdenas (1934–1940) listening to the Indians' requests.
Photographer unknown.

José Vasconcelos, paladin of the raza cósmica. Photo courtesy of the Nettie Lee Benson Latin American Collection, General Libraries, University of Texas at Austin.

Statue in Mexico City commemorating Cuitlahuac, defender of Tenochtitlán
against Cortéz. Photo courtesy of the Nettie Lee Benson Latin American
Collection, General Libraries, University of Texas at Austin.

output is so high in relation to their limited consumption of food."[91] If this is mild stuff, Gamio had no doubt that some of his fellow *indigenistas* went much further in propounding both racial differences and even racial hierarchies (with the old racist assumptions reversed). He reproved those who "preach and practice *indigenismo*, [who] limitlessly exalt the faculties of the Indian and consider him superior to the European in respect of intellectual and physical aptitudes."[92]

Again, examples of such reverse racism are not difficult to find, some focusing on the mestizo, some on the Indian. In the 1920s the mestizo carried off the palm. Cabrera argued that the dominance of the mestizo in Mexico derived inevitably from his superior adaptation to Mexican conditions. Vasconcelos wove an entire theory around the presumed virtues of hybridism (a deliberate riposte to Spencer), virtues that manifested themselves in the Mexican mestizo, the representative of the "cosmic race" ("By virtue of my race the spirit shall speak" was the motto Vasconcelos gave to the new autonomous national university). Hybridism, Vasconcelos argued, "tends to produce better types," since it blends different races possessing different qualities ("some races chiefly develop artistic ability; other people [*sic*] develop commercial aptitude; and so on"); thus—and here comes the familiar appeal to consensus—"the advantages of a mixture of races . . . have been generally recognized." The Mexican mestizo is a new biological product, the happy result of Spain's "superior" (i.e., miscegenating) colonial model.[93]

Similar "racial" explanations can be culled from the writings of revolutionaries like Salvador Alvarado, who saw world history as a racial struggle, with Mexico tied to the white race by "bonds of blood and ideals."[94] The automatic use of "race" as a rhetorical or explanatory device is evident in the discourse of key figures: Manuel Gómez Morín, Marte Gómez, Francisco Múgica, Lázaro Cárdenas.[95] Philosophers like Samuel Ramos, while echoing the standard denials of racial inequality, still resorted to "race" as a fundamental concept, still imputed attributes to "races," and still explained historical trends in "racial" terms (thus: "Our race lacks neither intelligence or vitality"; "the Spanish characteristics of our race have undergone important modifications"—its "primal energy" being dissipated in the "isolation of Mexico"; the Indian, "naturally inclined to passivity," lapsed into "Egyptianism"— a kind of torpid inertia, and the Indian "has influenced the soul of the other Mexican group, because he has mixed his blood with theirs").[96] Note that in these contexts "race" is not being used simply as a loose surrogate for ethnicity, and therefore we are not just disputing an inappropriate nomenclature: rather, "race" here carries connotations of innate, including biological, characteristics, determined at birth and subject only to long, slow processes of change.

By the 1930s, with radical *indigenismo* at its apogee, reverse racism focused on the Indian rather than on the mestizo. For some, the Indian represented "the most perfect moral and physical entity of our population"; Indians were "almost perfect, biologically speaking," and they possessed "a power of intellectual assimilation much greater, without comparison, than that of the white man"; thus, for example, "when he hates, [the Indian] hates with all the force conferred by his perfect organic constitution."[97] The Chamulas of Chiapas, reported a sympathizer, were a "strong race, not at all degenerate . . . lacking any hereditary disease, and almost pure, since there is very little or no admixture of white blood."[98] Ramón P. De Negri, painting a Spenglerian picture of Western decadence, saw hope in the Indian: "Biologically the Mexican Indian is more perfect than any of the other so-called colored races that exist in other continents; and in many cases equal or superior to the so-called whites."[99] The radical Indianists of the 1970s, whose reverse racism and anti-Westernism have already been noted, thus had a significant precursor group forty years earlier.

Although these examples testify to the continued strength of "racial" ideas and theories, even on the part of self-consciously antiracist activists, it should be noted that the bases of supposed racial attribution were tending to shift. Innate biological traits were still often stressed, as we have seen. But these traits were now also linked to environment and history, and the precise interrelationship of these different determinants often remained obscure. We have seen that Gamio, Molina Enríquez, and others alternated "race" and "class" with apparent intellectual abandon. Gamio made much of diet, physique, and environment; for Cabrera, the superiority of the mestizo was a question of superior environmental adaptation.[100] An alternative approach stressed mentality or collective psychology: the problem of the Indian (his "Egyptianism," in Ramos' phrase) derived from his long, collective acquaintance with conquest and oppression.

On the face of it, both of these formulations represent breaks with, and advances on, strict biological racism. For some critics, therefore, these would not be "racist" formulations, for the determination of supposed collective attributes has here shifted from genetics to geography and history.[101] But I do not think it is as simple as that. As John Rex has noted, a deemphasis on genetic determinism does not necessarily eliminate racism: "We should not take the disappearance of the specifically biologically oriented theories of race that were so important in the 1930s to mean that the class of sociological problems to which they referred has disappeared. Other deterministic theories would still be used and the essential distinguishing feature of this class of situations, namely, inequality between men being justified in a deterministic way, would still be present." According to this alternative view, racism may be discerned wherever "the inequalities and differentiation inherent in a social structure are related to physical and cultural criteria of an ascriptive kind and are rationalised in terms of deterministic belief systems."[102] The key terms here are *ascriptive* and *deterministic*. To equate ethnicity and race, and to suppose that they determine significant ascribed characteristics of such strength and staying power that they are, in practical terms, immutable, is to fall prey to racism, even if those characteristics are not alleged to be biologically determined. In other words, if Mexican Indians are what they are because of environmental pressures—and what they are scarcely admits of change, since it is part of their very being—then the question of whether biological, environmental, or historical factors determined this being is secondary. It is the inescapable ascription that counts.

Alfonso Caso, for example, who stresses the mutability—the capacity for acculturation—of the Indian, largely avoids this pitfall. Yet even he detects in the Indian a "marvelous intuition [*sic*] for the transformation of the crudest materials into beautiful artifacts."[103] In contrast, other *indigenistas*—and, today, Indianists—go much further, readily imputing a collective psychology, distinctively Indian, the product of centuries of oppression, transmitted through generations. In its more extreme forms, this theory makes Indians the carriers of a kind of Jungian collective unconscious no less determinant of their being than the old biological imperatives. And, given that racism involves the imputation of such ascribed and immutable characteristics, such psychological determinism seems to me to be racist, as was its biological predecessor.

Again, early manifestations of this psychological determinism appear in Gamio, who recurrently invokes the "traditionalist spirit of the [Indian] race, the faithful guardian of the memory of its glories and miseries." Like most of these psychological theorists, Gamio both homogenizes the Indian (all Indians share a common mental make-up) and also lays great stress on the common trauma of the Conquest. In the breast of the Indian is mixed "the vigor of the wild Tarahumara . . . the Athenian refinement of the divine Teotihuacano, the wisdom of the family of Tlaxcala, the unbending valor of the bloody Aztec"; yet all contemporary Indians are held back—not by innate, biological impediments—but rather by their ancient "intellectual baggage," which has condemned them to live "four hundred years behind the times, because their intellectual accomplishments are no more than a prolongation of those developed in pre-Hispanic times, and recast by the force of circumstances and environment."[104]

A similar theme runs through Ramos' psychological portrait of the Mexican (where debts to Spengler and Jung are acknowledged). While questioning crude biological racism, Ramos contrasts the "Faustian" spirit displayed by the "white sector" of the population with the passive, inert, anti-technological spirit of the Indians: "Mexican Indians are psychologically incapable of accepting technology, because . . . they lack the will to power; they do not belong to the race [*sic*] of rapacious men"; indeed, more generally, "the colored races do not possess the spirit to dominate." In Mexico's case, this inertia derives from a "collective conscience which is steeped and consolidated in its traditions," which, in turn, trace back to the trauma of the Conquest. The latter Ramos interprets—in a grotesque misapplication of psychoanalytic theory—as the formative childhood experience which "projected the evolution of the Mexican soul into a determined orbit." Indian inertia may, therefore, be historically and psychologically—not strictly biologically—determined, but it is nonetheless deterministically inescapable. Indeed, its transmission through generations appears to follow biological imperatives that defeat attempts at change or reform: "Superior to man's will is a biological law which precludes any fundamental suppression of the past."[105]

Such psychological determinism, with its bizarre borrowings from Freud and Jung, has remained a staple of *indigenista*—and Indianist—thought. Marroquín, offering a milder version, sees the Indian as "a socioeconomic category historically conditioned ever since the Spanish conquest," since that involved "a psychological trauma . . . transmitted to [the Indians'] descendants."[106] And the radical Indianists of recent years have reworked the theme, stressing the "collective memory" of the Indian, and the latent "residues" that must be recovered and utilized in the reconstruction of the Indianist utopia.[107] Nor is the idea confined to intellectual theories. A *político* landlord of the Valle del Mezquital observes: 'The Indian is a completely isolated type . . . [who] carries the complex of the epoch of the Conquest."[108] It should be stressed that this quasi-Jungian psychological attribution is not only deterministic (imputing to all Indians a common, ineluctable psyche), but also unproven, and probably unprovable. Empirical evidence points to the great gulf—of historical experience and cultural transformation—which separates twentieth-century Mexican Indians from their supposed sixteenth-century forebears, and which consigns any notion of a collective psychological inheritance to the realm of metaphysics. [109]

Revolutionary *indigenismo*—and, later, Indianism—thus embodied assumptions that were, arguably, racist. In some (moderate) cases, racism was an intellectual encumbrance that could not be shaken off; it stood as testimony to the continuities linking Porfirian and revolutionary thought. In other cases, reverse racism developed by way of reaction against Porfirian prejudices. In almost all cases, too, the positive rehabilitation—or even exaltation—of the Indian and mestizo carried negative implications for other "races": that is, the racist tendencies of *indigenismo*/Indianism manifested themselves—logically—in derogations of non-Indian or mestizo "races." Here, the potential evidence is abundant, but it is not always easy to establish whether *indigenista* antipathies to blacks, Spaniards, North Americans, or Chinese are strictly racist, or merely nationalist.

The United States, for example, figured as a bugbear of much revolutionary nationalist *indigenista* thought. Just as Sierra had urged nation-building in order to counter the looming threat of the United States, so Gamio, who was no outright xenophobe, deplored the Americanization of Baja California ("absolutely exotic, Yankeefied") and expressed confidence that Protestantism ("abstract, exotic, iconoclastic, and incomprehensible") could never appeal to Mexico's Indians.[110] Vasconcelos argued that North Americans and Latin Americans, being offspring of different "parental races," revealed contrasting "racial, temperamental and spiritual differences"; later, as he shifted right, he penned yet more bitter diatribes against the United States, denouncing both *pochismo* (the hybrid U.S./Mexican culture of Northern Mexico) and pro-Americanism, that "Saxonism, which disguises itself with the cosmetic of the most deficient civilization which history has known."[111]

Generally, however, North Americans escaped racist—as against political or cultural—deprecation, and other ethnic groups, more readily stigmatized, bore the brunt. Molina Enríquez, keen to rehabilitate the mestizo, had no time for blacks; for some enthusiastic *indigenistas*, the necessary corollary of rehabilitating the Indians was sweeping, "systematic" condemnation of Spaniards, the hated *gachupines*.[112]

But the clearest example of xenophobia, undoubtedly racist and, I suggest, functionally related to *indigenista* nationalism, was Sinophobia.

During and after the Revolution, Mexico's Chinese population was subjected to sustained persecution, which led to mass expulsions in 1931.[113] The background can be quickly sketched. Chinese immigration to Mexico, actively encouraged by the Díaz government, had never been extensive—the total Chinese population in 1910 was probably less than 40,000—but it was sufficient to create sizeable colonies in certain states, especially in Northwestern Mexico.[114] During the late Porfiriato, anti-Chinese sentiment surfaced, but it was not until the Revolution that it reached major proportions, evident in both popular violence and official policy. During the years of fighting, 1910–1920, the Chinese were repeatedly intimidated, attacked, robbed, and murdered. Over two hundred died in a single pogrom at Torreón in May 1911.[115] There is no doubt that anti-Chinese feeling, while permitted and often encouraged by the authorities, had genuine popular roots. And, during the 1920s, politicians courted support by advocating, and implementing, anti-Chinese measures: economic controls, taxes, ghettoization, and ultimately expulsion. Such campaigns were conducted with all the panoply of xenophobic racism. The Chinese were stereotyped as filthy, disease-ridden, money-grubbing, parasitic, and sexually threatening. They spread sickness, gambling and drug-addiction. In the face of this "Chinese flood," Mexican patriots had to "heal the country of this grave evil" which was "corrupting the organism of our race."[116]

Several aspects of revolutionary Sinophobia deserve emphasis. First, it possessed a clear economic rationale. The Chinese, originally brought into the country to provide cheap labor, soon became highly successful shopkeepers, traders, and businessmen, especially in the booming Northwest. In particular, they established a profitable symbiotic liaison with the big U.S. mining companies, such as the Cananea Company, for whom they provided many of the basic retailing services and, in doing so, squeezed out Mexican competitors.[117] They also sold to the urban poor, which made them vulnerable to popular and populist attacks, especially when times were hard. The circumstances were therefore appropriate for the growth of what Van den Berghe terms "competitive" racism—racism that, in terms of its socioeconomic rationale, differed from the racism that had historically afflicted Mexico's Indians.[118]

But Sinophobia also embodied a range of powerful "irrational" prejudices, which served to legitimize persecution and to lend it "theoretical" justification. Like Europe's Jews, the Chinese were seen as both parasitic and idle, yet also industrious and overly successful. They spread disease (trachoma and beriberi), encouraged vice (opium addiction and gambling), and debauched Mexican womanhood (Chinese immigration had been overwhelmingly male). Thus, they prostituted the Mexican "race." Images of tentacular octopuses and corrupt blood, of contagious disease and exotic perversion, accompanied the anti-Chinese campaigns. Damned if they miscegenated, the Chinese were damned if they didn't; their separateness— "otherness"—gave rise to bizarre speculations and fantasies, which focused on the

Chinese' secret societies, their cloistered rituals, their penchant for poisoning. The Torreón pogrom was triggered by a supposed poisoning of revolutionaries by devious Chinese; the death of the great Sonoran Chinese-baiter, José María Arana, was attributed to Chinese poisoners.[119] Even today, stories redolent of medieval anti-Semitism concerning the abduction and ritual murder of Mexican infants by Chinese are told in Northern Mexico.[120] The parallels with European anti-Semitism do not need to be labored. Here was a "racial" group (one that was somatically more recognizable than Jews, furthermore), engaged in successful economic competition with the Mexican petite bourgeoisie, a class which supplied many of the new revolutionary leaders of the 1920s. Here, too, was a group lacking powerful diplomatic protection, against whom the populist nationalism of the Revolution could be safely vented. Thus, just as that nationalism sought to "forge the nation" by integrating the Indian, so it also sought to cleanse the nation by expelling the Chinese (since integration, in this case, would mean racial surrender and decline). Sinophobia was the logical corollary of revolutionary *indigenismo*. And the outcome, in Mexico as in Europe, was discriminatory legislation, ghettoization, and expulsion.[121]

The final point to stress is the functional interdependence of *indigenista* nationalism and Sinophobia. That is not to say that all *indigenista* nationalists were Sinophobes or vice versa, but that the two were logically related, and, in fact, coexisted in the theory and practice of certain groups, notably the revolutionary nationalists (rather than, say, their conservative Catholic enemies). The first coherent statement of Sinophobia was the work of the Partido Liberal Mexicano, radical opponents of Díaz in the 1900s. The Sonorans who battled to national power in the following decade were also carriers of Sinophobia. Salvador Alvarado, eager to uplift the Indian and to modernize Mexico, not least by the promotion of immigration, was adamant that no Chinese should be admitted to the country: "Asiatics are in no respect . . . suitable, neither to improve our race, nor to increase and develop our resources. They never assimilate. They remain Asiatics and are in effect leeches sucking the money from our country"; those already in Mexico should be subjected to "the most severe sanitary regulations and should be directed to districts outside the cities where they might reside."[122] In the Northwest, a vigorous movement "in defence of the race," which claimed five thousand members drawn from all social classes, called for similar measures against the Chinese.[123] And, with Calles, the Sonoran archnationalist, in the presidency, their wishes were progressively gratified. Regulation and discrimination increased, culminating in mass expulsions in 1931.[124] Thereafter, their target eliminated or much reduced, the Sinophobes quietened. Interestingly, however, the years immediately after were marked by a rising, vocal anti-Semitism, which emanated from similar sociopolitical circles: the petty-bourgeois revolutionaries who, having entered upon power and flaunted their nationalist credentials through the 1920s, now, in the economically depressed, ideologically innovative 1930s, sought to defend their notion of the Revolution—nationalist, capitalist, racist—in the face of new radical movements.[125]

I began this discussion of race and revolution with a brief outline of race relations on the eve of the Revolution. Against this backdrop I discussed revolutionary theories and motives, noting how the revolutionaries, consciously reacting against Porfirian ideology, sought a nationalist incorporation of the Indian but how, in doing so, they tended to perpetuate alternative, subtler forms of racism. It cannot be denied, however, that the official ideology of the regime thoroughly repudiated the old, "Westernist," Eurocentric racism and that this represented a significant change. But how significant was the change in society at large? How were practical race relations affected by this formal, maybe "superstructural," reassessment? I cannot adequately answer so complex and intangible a question, but I can suggest some rough conclusions.

Postrevolutionary Race Relations

Some authorities, we have seen, deny the existence of racism in postrevolutionary Mexico, crediting, in part, the conscious exhortatory efforts of the regime.[126] But the antiracist rhetoric of national elites cannot be taken as sufficient proof. Racism can be driven underground (not necessarily very far underground); it can shift its premises (e.g., from biological to other, ostensibly more plausible, determinants) without that ideological shift substantially affecting its daily practice; and daily practice may even acquire added virulence as a result of official attempts at positive discrimination.

It is certainly true that the Revolution further accelerated the breakdown of castelike ethnic barriers, speeding Mexico's transition to a society fully stratified along class lines; by 1970, with only 8 percent of the population linguistically classified as "Indian," Mexico was approaching the status of a "monoethnic mestizo nation."[127] In this, as in other respects, Molina Enríquez stands as an inspired prophet.[128] This outcome, however, owed less to government action ("the Revolution" as conscious policy) than to the unplanned consequences of revolutionary upheaval (war, social and spatial mobility, the making and breaking of fortunes) and the rapid economic development which the Revolution helped encourage over time (in short, "the Revolution" as unconscious process). Government efforts to educate and uplift the Indian population achieved only modest success.[129] In contrast, massive labor migration—national and international—and rapid urbanization, have both served to break down the old "regions of refuge" and to acquaint Indian groups with wage labor, Spanish, literacy, and political activism.[130] Incidentally, this has not invariably resulted in the "de-Indianization" which latter-day Indianists deplore; the old revolutionary *indigenistas* were right to suggest that acculturation *could* proceed without the inevitable destruction of Indian culture and identity.[131]

The secular decline of castelike ethnic barriers—assumed by many to be "racial"—thus proceeded apace, accelerated by the Revolution; and the social space in which racist beliefs and practices prevailed consequently tended to contract (we could phrase this less optimistically: other forms of inequality and prejudice held sway in their place). But racism did not wither on the vine. Against the confident obituaries of Mexican racism already cited, we could set more sombre estimates of an "omnipresent dimension" of racism in Mexican society, or of a "profoundly racist ideology" which, according to one analysis, underpins the rule of both traditional rural caciques and also newer "liberal technocratic" regional bourgeoisies.[132]

It may be hypothesized, first, that the very elimination of castelike ethnic barriers produced a racist reaction. In some areas, it is clear (though the subject has been little researched) that the political mobilization of Indian groups, their conquest of limited political or economic gains, their acquisition of new skills, all provoked a Ladino backlash. Especially in "regions of refuge," where ethnic relations had retained a more archaic, quasi-colonial form, the transition to a more open, less ascriptive society displayed some of the features of Van den Berghe's "competitive" racism—which, I have argued, underpinned popular Sinophobia. But whereas Sinophobia could boldly trumpet its message since it was legitimized by the regime, Ladino racism had to remain more mute and circumspect, as it clashed with official norms. Nevertheless, it is clear that white and mestizo victims of caste erosion denounced Indian uppishness and sought to counter it, reasserting their traditional "racial" (i.e., ethnic) superiority. Landlords lamented the postrevolutionary insouciance of once-docile Indians; lower-class mestizos (the racist constituency Van den Berghe would emphasize) cleaved to their eroding ethnic privilege. At Dzitas (Yucatán), the Indians had "got out of their place," securing political office and "no longer, by gesture and manner of speech, indicat[ing] that respect for *vecinos* which old *vecinos* regard as their due"; in response, the *vecinos* clung doggedly to their sole social asset—Spanish surname and lineage.[133] Down to the present, in Indian zones, one hears the (mestizo) comment that "the Indian who frees himself is dangerous . . . if he enters respectable circles [*el medio cultural*] without dominating himself he is a bad character; and if he manages to dominate himself, he becomes a protector of his own kind."[134]

The erosion of "regions of refuge"—the classic Indian zones, especially of the South—has tended to swell, relatively, the number of acculturated Indians: the "Indo-mestizos" of Molina Enríquez and "folk" peoples of Redfield and Eyler Simpson, groups that are more bilingual, more integrated into the national economy and politics, yet still ethnically "Indian" (in terms, for example, of dress, religion, "cargo," and *compadrazgo* systems). Indeed, the Revolution has tended to foster this development by means of *indigenista* policy, agrarian reform, and rural education. From the 1920s to the present, allegedly "Indian" values have been officially exalted. Official policy has produced the great showpiece of Indian culture and, according to the logic of revolutionary *indigenismo*, the "monument to Mexican nationalism," namely, Mexico City's Museum of Anthropology; it has encouraged a romantic valorization of "Indian" arts and crafts, dance and music (witness the Ballet Folklórico); it has created symbolic constructs like the Plaza of the Three Cultures at Tlatelolco.[135] Latter-day "cultural extremists," we have seen, seek to go even further in exalting Indianness.

Yet there is a paradox at the heart of such policies. The Indians whose culture is valorized and whose emancipation is proclaimed find themselves once again in the position of reacting to an imposed ideology. Their reaction is utilitarian: they exploit whatever opportunities official *indigenismo* confers, even playing up to their exotic or romantic official image. At Hueyapan, villagers "put on an ethnic show" for a visiting gubernatorial candidate, complete with ersatz Indian garb and Nahuatl script.[136] In the Valle del Mezquital, Otomí political bosses use Indian identity in order to maintain ethnic marginality and traditional *caciquista* authority.[137] In Michoacán, Indianness becomes a useful political weapon for hardheaded Tarascan caciques engaged in rough power-politics. In this last case, it is clear, ethnicity represents a political option more than an ascriptive inevitability.[138]

Official ideology, we may say, has thus perpetuated a kind of instrumental Indianness. But this Indianness stands at odds with social reality. For perceptions of Indian inferiority still permeate society, official ideology notwithstanding. White/mestizo deprecation of supposed Indian attributes keeps alive the old pattern of negative Indian identification: "to be Indian in Hueyapan is to have a primarily negative identity"; Indians, in other words, are still defined in terms not of positive attributes but rather of negative failings—lack of education, of fluency in Spanish, of shoes or baths or other material possessions.[139] And, as in the past, these criteria constantly shift, as Mexican society itself changes, creating new cultural desiderata.

A whole range of prejudices and discriminations therefore exists, but exists in defiance of official ideology. Indian languages are officially endorsed, unofficially frowned upon. Naranjeños "assert that they know Tarascan too, or express guilt when their language is faulty. On the other hand, monolingual Tarascans from Acajo are scoffed at and many people avoid using the indigenous tongue for fear of being mocked as 'Indians' in the streets."[140] So, too, with dress: an Indian woman spurns the traditional skirt "because her husband did not want her or his daughters to dress like 'Indians'."[141] And religion: Agustín Gómez, a member of one of Oscar Lewis' "five families," "was of the opinion that [his wife] Rosa was more backward and 'Indian' than he in religious matters," since she skimped on Catholic ritual.[142]

The ancient practice of "whitening" also continues, reinforced by film, television, and advertising stereotypes. The aesthetic preferences of earlier literary elites ("You find almost in every one of our Indian or mestizo poets, dark of skin themselves, the ardent eulogy of the white hands, the pale cheek, of the *amada*," Vasconcelos observed) become the stock-in-trade of today's soap operas.[143] Naranja witnessed the "romantic suicide of a girl whose mother would not let her marry a nephew of Primo Tapia [the Indian *agrarista*] because he, the nephew, was 'too Indian'." The Naranja caciques, in fact, have tended to practice ethnic exogamy (so, too, have Mexican presidents; no president, I am reliably told, has ever married a woman darker than himself).[144]

Above all, Indians have remained subject to informal discrimination, based on anti-Indian prejudice, which is rooted in the subsoil of Mexican culture. The people of Hueyapan are "acutely aware of still being Indians, for they are constantly so designated by outsiders."[145] In the Sierra de Puebla, mestizos are still the self-styled *gente de razón* (respectable folk), Nahuatl-speaking Indians are *coyotes*.[146] Other pejorative terms abound, not least *indio* and *indito*: there are no *indios* in Mérida, Redfield commented in the 1930s, "except as the term becomes an epithet addressed to any low-class person, especially if dark in complexion or rude in behavior."[147] The practice has not died. In the Valle del Mezquital, for example, much of the old grass-roots racism lives on: the Otomí "have always been negligent . . . they are difficult people, stubborn by nature of their race"; "they're half-mules, they lack training"; "the Otomí is a person backward by nature." And, again, we encounter the lazy native: "the chief problem that most of the dominant class cite is that of the apathy, idleness, and boorishness of the Indian population."[148]

It is worth adding that the Valle de Mezquital data do not reveal a uniform attachment to strict biological racism on the part of non-Indians; rather, biological racism consorts with vaguer imputations of Indian backwardness, which for some is environmentally determined, for some corrigible by means of education. To that extent, perhaps, official *indigenismo* may have left a mark. But the weight of evidence supports the contention made earlier, in more abstract terms: that is, the demise of biological racism by no means spells the end of racism, which may be predicated upon other deterministic factors, and which is likely to survive, irrespective of shifts in official ideology, so long as sociopolitical circumstances are propitious.

The conflict between official ideology and sociopolitical circumstances leaves Indians—still victims of externally imposed categories—caught in a dilemma. Official ideology proclaims their worth, even their superiority (hence the phenomenon of instrumental *indigenismo*); but sociopolitical circumstances repeatedly display the reality of prejudice. Indians "are discriminated against for being Indian and at the same time admired for being the 'real soul' of Mexico, living proof of Mexico's noble pre-Hispanic heritage."[149] The dilemma is apparent at both the individual and the collective levels, and one recurrent consequence, at the latter level, is the frequent polarization of Indian communities not according to conventional political criteria of Left and Right but rather in terms of a conflict between modernizers and traditionalists, between those who ally with the forces of acculturation and those who cleave to tradition, between those who, in the Tepoztlán of the 1920s, were known as the *correctos* and those who were denoted *tontos*.[150]

Official *indigenismo* may thus have softened—or at least silenced—some of the earlier excesses of full-fledged biological racism. But it contained its own contradictions, which led it to devise racist formulae of its own, and it wrestled with an intractably racist society. There can be no doubt that racism has declined since the days of Díaz, but that decline has been principally the result of rapid acculturation, spurred by social upheaval and economic development. The "Indian problem" has become more manageable chiefly because the number of Indians has declined, certainly relatively; and, one might add, because alternative problems have become more acute. But where Indians remain, racism remains, and government fiat can no more eliminate racism in Mexico than it can in Britain or the United States. Government fiat is a necessary but far from sufficient condition for its elimination. The racial theorists of the Porfiriato may have been relegated to dusty bookshelves, but the daily practice that their theories rationalized continues. And it is likely to continue until either the sociopolitical circumstances that nurture it are radically changed, or Indian ethnic identity is rendered socially neutral, that is, until ethnically patterned forms of subordination are completely replaced by class relations, a process that is well advanced, but still far from complete. If radical change does not solve the "Indian problem," continued "development" will eventually remove it altogether.

Notes

1. All four were prolific writers as well as active administrators. Basic careers were as follows. Manuel Gamio (1883–1960): pioneer anthropologist and archaeologist; undersecretary of education,1925; first director of the Interamerican Indigenista Institute (1942–1960); considered "the true pioneer of modern indigenismo in Mexico and the Continent" (*Diccionario Porrúa de Historia, Biografía, y Geografía de México* [Mexico, Editorial Porrúa, 1986], p. 1143). José Vasconcelos (1881–1959): philosopher, revolutionary intellectual, and political activist; director of the National University; secretary of education (1921–1924); unsuccessful presidential candidate, 1929; director of the Biblioteca de México, 1940. Alfonso Caso (1896–1970): archaeologist and *indigenista*; excavator of Monte Albán; director of the National Museum, 1933–1934, of the National Preparatory School, 1938, and of the National Institute of Anthropology and History, 1939–1944; rector of the National University, 1944–1945. Gonzalo Aguirre Beltrán (b.1908): physician; director of *indigenista* affairs, Department of Education, 1946–1952; federal deputy, Veracruz, 1961–1964; director-general, National Indigenista Institute, 1971–1972.

2. José Vasconcelos, *La raza cósmica, misión de la raza iberoamericana* (Paris: Agencia Mundial de Librería, 1925); Andrés Molina Enríquez, *Los grandes problemas nacionales* (Mexico: A. Carranza, 1909).

3. Pierre L.Van den Berghe, *Race and Racism: A Comparative Perspective* (New York: Wiley, 1967), pp. 55–56.

4. Ashley Montagu, *Race, Science and Humanity* (New York: Van Nostrand Reinhold, 1963), p. iii.

5. John Rex, "The Concept of Race in Sociological Theory," in Sami Zubaida, ed., *Race and Racialism* (London: Tavistock Publications, 1970), pp. 37–38.

6. Frank B. Livingstone, "On the non-existence of human races," in Ashley Montagu, ed., *The Concept of Race* (New York: Free Press of Glencoe, 1964), pp. 46–60; Stephen Jay Gould, *Ever Since Darwin: Reflections in Natural History* (Harmondsworth: Penguin Books, 1986), ch. 8, pt. A.

7. Gonzalo Aguirre Beltrán, *La población negra de México, 1519–1810* (Mexico: Ediciones Fuente Cultural, 1946).

8. In the jargon of genetics, such "nomenclatural stasis" could not handle a "patently dynamic system": Gould, *Ever Since Darwin*, p. 236. Anselmo Marino Flores, "Indian Population and Its Identification," in Manning Nash, ed., *Handbook of Middle American Indians*, VI, *Social Anthropology* (Austin: University of Texas Press, 1975), p. 14; Gonzalo Aguirre Beltrán, *Obra polémica* (Mexico: Instituto Nacional de Antropología e Historia, 1976), p. 127.

9. Richard J. Salvucci, *Textiles and Capitalism in Mexico: An Economic History of the Obrajes, 1539–1840* (Princeton: Princeton University Press, 1987), p. 18.

10. Enrique Krauze, *Porfirio Díaz* (Mexico: Fondo de Cultura Económica, 1987), p. 8; Alan Knight, *The Mexican Revolution*, 2 vols. (Cambridge: Cambridge University Press, 1986), I: pp. 3–4. The source is an American, although an American who had lived in Mexico for twenty-four years, and whose views would have tallied with those of elite Mexicans.

11. Hence the old adage, "Money whitens." F. Fuenzalida, cited by Françoise Morin, "Indien, indigenisme, indianité," in *Indianité, ethnocide, indigenisme en Amérique Latine* (Paris: Editions du Centre National de la Recherche Scientifique, 1982), p. 4.

12. Robert Redfield, *The Folk Culture of Yucatan* (Chicago: University of Chicago Press, 1950), pp. 13, 79; Paul Friedrich, *The Princes of Naranja: An Essay in Anthrohistorical Method* (Austin: University of Texas Press, 1986), p. 185.

13. Hugo G. Nuttini and Betty Bell, *Ritual Kinship: The Structure and Historical Development of the Compadrazgo System in Rural Tlaxcala*, 2 vols. (Princeton: Princeton University Press, 1980), I: p. 13.

14. Manuel Gamio, *Forjando patria* (1916; reprint, Mexico: Editorial Porrúa, 1960), pp. 171–181.

15. Ibid., pp. 9, 171–181; Gonzalo Aguirre Beltrán, "Prólogo" to Alfonso Caso, *La comunidad indígena* (Mexico: Secretaría de Educación Pública, 1971), p. 20.

16. F. Rodríguez Cabo to Departamento de Trabajo, 30 September 1935, Archivo General de la Nación, Presidentes, Lázaro Cárdenas, 533.4/12 (henceforth: AGN/LC); Guillermo Bonfil Batalla, *Utopia y revolución: El pensamiento político contemporáneo de los indios en América Latina* (Mexico: Editorial Nueva Imagen, 1981), p. 21.

17. Judith Friedlander, *Being Indian in Hueyapan: A Study of Forced Identity in Contemporary Mexico* (New York: St. Martin's Press, 1975), p. 77.

18. Oscar Lewis, *Pedro Martínez: A Mexican Peasant and His Family* (London: Panther Books, 1969), p. 28; see also Gregory G. Reck, *In the Shadow of Tlaloc: Life in a Mexican Village* (Harmondsworth: Penguin Books, 1978), p. 57.

19. Alejandro Marroquín, *Balance del indigenismo. Informe sobre la política indígena en América Latina* (Mexico: Instituto Indigenista Interamericano, 1972), p. 8.

20. Caso, *La comunidad indígena*, pp. 10–11, 89–90.

21. Friedlander, *Being Indian*, pp. 72–73.

22. Bonfil Batalla, *Utopia y revolución*, p. 19. On which, see Guillermo de la Peña, "Orden social y educación indígena en México: la pervivencia de un legado colonial," in Susana Glantz, ed., *La heterodoxia recuperada: en torno a Angel Palerm* (Mexico: Fondo de Cultura Ecónomica, 1987), pp. 286–299.

23. Ida Altman and James Lockhart, eds., *Provinces of Early Mexico: Variants of Spanish American Regional Evolution* (Berkeley: University of California Press, 1976), p. 99; William Taylor, *Drink, Homicide and Rebellion in Colonial Mexican Villages* (Stanford: Stanford University Press, 1979).

24. Eyler N. Simpson, *The Ejido: Mexico's Way Out* (Chapel Hill: University of North Carolina Press, 1937), p. 243; Friedlander, *Being Indian*, pp. 83–100.

25. Paul Friedrich, *Agrarian Revolt in a Mexican Village* (Chicago: University of Chicago Press, 1977), pp. 47, 51; John Womack, Jr., *Zapata and the Mexican Revolution* (New York: Vintage Books, 1969), p. 243.

26. Womack, *Zapata*, pp. 100–102, 142; Gamio, *Forjando patria*, pp. 176–177. An indication of Gamio's misguided understanding of Zapatismo comes with his appreciation of that revolutionary who has "most sensibly grasped the Zapatista problem and conceived adequate measures to resolve it"—namely, the corrupt scourge of Morelos, Pablo González, p. 181.

27. Claude Bataillon, "Note sur l'indigenisme au Méxique," in Morin, *Indianité* (see n.11), p. 93.

28. Gamio, *Forjando patria*, pp. 93, 174; Marroquín, *Balance*, p. 59.

29. "*Indigenismo* represents neither the ideology of the Indian nor of the Spaniard, but rather that of the mestizo": Gonzalo Aguirre Beltrán, "The Indian and the Mexican Revolution," lecture, University of Texas, n.d., p. 1.

30. Gamio, *Forjando patria*, pp. 22, 25, 94–95.

31. Van den Berghe, *Race and Racism*, pp. 29, 55; Moisés González Navarro, "Mestizaje in Mexico in the Nineteenth Century," in Magnus Mörner, ed., *Race and Class in Latin America* (New York: Columbia University Press, 1971), pp. 145–155.

32. Rodolfo Stavenhagen, "México: minorías étnicas y política cultural," *Nexos* 19, July 1979, p. 13. Note also Rex's critique of Oliver C. Cox's class-reductionist thesis, "The Concept of Race," p. 42, and Jorge Hernández Díaz, "Relaciones interétnicas contemporáneas en Oaxaca," in Alicia M. Barabas and Miguel A. Bartolomé, eds., *Etnicidad y pluralismo cultural: La dinámica étnica en Oaxaca* (Mexico: Instituto Nacional de Antropología e Historia, 1986), pp. 310–315.

33. Aguirre Beltrán, *Obra polémica*, pp. 35–40; Arnaldo Córdova, *La ideologia de la revolución mexicana:La formación del nuevo régimen* (Mexico: Ediciones Era, 1973), pp. 53–54, 63–64; Moisés González Navarro, *Historia moderna de México: El Porfiriato, la vida social* (Mexico: Editorial Hermes, 1970), pp. 150–177.

34. Justo Sierra, *The Political Evolution of the Mexican People*, transl. Charles Ramsdell (Austin: University of Texas Press, 1969), p. 368.

35. Syed Hussein Alatas, *The Myth of the Lazy Native* (London: Frank Cass, 1977); Alan Knight, "Mexican Peonage: What Was It and Why Was It?," *Journal of Latin American Studies,* 18 (1986): 55–56; and note the interesting educational examples given by Mary Kay Vaughan, *The State, Education and Social Class in Mexico, 1880–1928* (DeKalb: Northern Illinois University Press, 1982), pp. 26–29.

36. Knight, *Mexican Revolution,* I: 88; Womack, *Zapata,* p. 41.

37. Knight, "Mexican Peonage," pp. 61–73.

38. Sierra, *Political Evolution,* pp. 352, 368.

39. Martin S. Stabb, "Indigenism and Racism in Mexican Thought, 1857–1911," *Journal of Inter-American Studies,* I (1959): 405–443; T. G. Powell, "Mexican Intellectuals and the Indian Question, 1876–1911," *Hispanic American Historical Review* 48 (1968): 19–36; William D. Raat, "Ideas and Society in Don Porfirio's Mexico," *The Americas* 30 (1973): pp. 32–53.

40. Vaughan, *The State,* ch. 2; De la Peña, "Orden social," pp. 306–307.

41. Frederick Starr, *In Indian Mexico: A Narrative of Travel and Labor* (Chicago: Forbes & Co., 1908), p. 100.

42. For a stimulating analysis of the tradition of elite *indigenismo,* see David Brading, *The Origins of Mexican Nationalism* (Cambridge: Centre of Latin American Studies, 1985).

43. Knight, *Mexican Revolution,* I: 10.

44. Héctor Aguilar Camín, *La frontera nómada: Sonora y la Revolución Mexicana* (Mexico: Siglo Veintiuno, 1985), pp. 59–66.

45. Knight, *Mexican Revolution,* I: 18; Womack, *Zapata,* pp. 41–42, 63. Recent scholarship has revealed, at the level of the state executives, a clear shift away from the popular, home-grown, caudillo-style governors of the early Porfiriato, to the more cosmopolitan, elitist, and "plutocratic" governors of the 1890s and 1900s. This shift, from populists to plutocrats, was associated with more openly contemptuous and racist elite attitudes: see Friedrich Katz, ed., *Porfirio Díaz frente al descontento popular regional, 1891–1893* (Mexico: Universidad Iberoamericana, 1986), p. 21, and F.-X. Guerra, *De l'Ancien Régime à la Révolution,* 2 vols. (Paris: Editions L'Harmattan, 1985), I: 94–95.

46. Caso, *La comunidad indígena,* p. 127.

47. *Diario de los debates del congreso constituyente, 1916–1917,* 2 vols. (Mexico: Talleres Gráficos de la Nación, 1960), I: 703. For a résumé of *indigenista* policy in the 1920s, see Simpson, *The Ejido,* ch. 16.

48. Gamio, *Forjando patria,* pp. 73, 175; Aguirre Beltrán, *Obra polémica,* p. 27; Caso, *La comunidad indígena,* pp. 47–52; and Aguirre Beltrán's prologue to Caso, *La comunidad indígena,* p. 23: "for Gamio as for Caso, archaeology in our country has, as its predominant practical function, that of supplying the Mexican with an identity, that is, with a root in the most remote past." David A. Brading, "Manuel Gamio and Official Indígenismo in Mexico," *Bulletin of Latin American Research* 7 (1988): 87–88, exaggerates Gamio's desire to "destroy the native culture which had emerged during the colonial period."

49. Programa de Acción del Departamento de Asuntos Indígenas, 10 September 1936, AGN/LC 545.2/5.

50. Aguirre Beltrán, "The Indian and the Mexican Revolution" (see n. 29).

51. Thus, on the one hand, Cárdenas stressed the need to give "great attention" to the Indian question (which, arguably, he did); yet at the same time he leaned to the "leftist Westernist" position, stating that "the program for the emancipation of the Indian is, in essence, that of the emancipation of the proletariat of any country, without forgetting the special conditions of his climate, past and needs, which give him a distinct physiognomy": Luis González, *Historia de la revolución mexicana, 1934–40. Los días del presidente Cárdenas* (Mexico: El Colegio de México, 1981), pp. 117–128.

52. Octavio Paz, *The Other Mexico: Critique of the Pyramid*, transl. Lysander Kemp (New York: Grove Press, 1972), p. 91.

53. Friedlander, *Being Indian*, pp. xv–xvi, and ch. 7.

54. Vicente Lombardo Toledano, *El problema del indio* (Mexico: Secretaría de Educación Pública, 1973), pp. 82, 94, 101; Aguirre Beltrán, prologue to Caso, *La comunidad indígena*, p. 27.

55. Aguirre Beltrán, prologue to Caso, *La comunidad indígena*, pp. 33–36, discusses van Zantwijk vs. Caso; and Aguirre Beltrán, *Obra polémica*, pp. 173–227, rebuts recent radical critiques of traditional *indigenismo* launched by those who denounce acculturation and assert the nationhood of Indian groups "whom *indigenista* ideology denies the right of a separate cultural existence" (p. 220).

56. Bonfil Batalla, *Utopia y revolución*, p. 30; Marie-Chantal Barre, *Ideologías indigenistas y movimientos indios* (Mexico: Siglo Veintiuno, 1983).

57. Luis Cabrera, "El balance de la revolución," in *La revolución es la revolución* (Guanajuato: Ediciones del Gobierno del Estado de Guanajuato, 1977), p. 282; Friedlander, *Being Indian*, pp. 166–167.

58. Gamio, *Forjando patria*, p. 159; Gonzalo Aguirre Beltrán, *Teoría y práctica de la educación indígena* (Mexico: Sepsetentas, 1973).

59. Friedlander, *Being Indian*, pp. 68, 129–131.

60. Ibid., pp. 135–136, 155; Gilbert M. Joseph, *Revolution from Without: Yucatán, Mexico and the United States, 1880–1924* (Cambridge: Cambridge University Press, 1982), pp. 220–224.

61. Cabrera, "El balance de la revolución," p. 281; Van den Berghe, *Race and Racism*, pp. 55–56; Caso, *La comunidad indígena*, p. 109.

62. Aline Helg,"The Idea of Race in Argentina, 1880–1930," unpublished paper, 1987, pp. 12, 66. For Mexico 1910 marked not only the centennial and the outbreak of the Revolution; it also signaled—so it has been argued—"the beginning of the contemporary period of Mexican thought," a break involving a rejection of positivism and "scientism," a turn toward idealism, mysticism, and Bergsonianism, and a certain emphasis on shared Latin American culture. The Ateneo de la Juventud (1909) is seen as the institutional pioneer of this intellectual shift which, while it had little direct connection to the Revolution, certainly lent encouragement to new

departures in political philosophy, such as *indigenismo*. See Patrick Romanell, *Making of the Mexican Mind* (Notre Dame: University of Notre Dame Press, 1971), pp. 56–66 and Enrique Krauze, *Caudillos culturales en la revolución mexicana* (Mexico: Siglo Veintiuno, 1976), p. 51.

63. See note 39.

64. Joseph, *Revolution from Without*, pp. 107–109; Thomas L. Benjamin, "Passages to Leviathan: Chiapas and the Mexican State, 1891–1947," PhD diss., Michigan State University, 1981, pp. 137–141. The response of revolutionary elites to their confrontation with "the Indian" varied. "In the hard struggle which we sustained against the soldiers of reaction," Gen. Felipe Dusart later recalled, "we were able to acquire a profound knowledge of the problem of our Indian race"; "fortunately," an academic concurred, "the violent phase of the Revolution brought about the exact and indisputable revelation that the Indian is an active force within our nationality" (Dusart speech, 18 October1935; Rafael Molina Betancourt to Cárdenas, "Al margen de las afirmaciones presidenciales sobre el problema social de la incorporación indígena en la vida nacional," 30 June 1936, both AGN/LC 545.3/147). But compare the contemporary opinion of Ciro B. Ceballos, a prominent Carrancista propagandist, who argued the beneficial consequences of the revolutionary triumph of the northerners (*los fronterizos*), unless it were to turn out that "on putting themselves in intimate contact with the rest of the Mexican population . . . the former [northerners] were to acquire the vices of the latter, leading to the degeneration, if not the transformation, of the essential conditions of their present indisputable racial superiority" (*El Demócrata,* 18 January 1916).

65. Salvador Alvarado to Carranza, 25 January 1916, in Isidro Fabela, *Documentos históricos de la revolución mexicana, revolución y régimen constitucionalista* 27 vols. (Mexico: Fondo de Cultura Ecónomica, 1960–1973) V: pp. 22–23.

66. Benjamin, "Passages to Leviathan," pp. 229–230.

67. Diéguez's exact words translate: "The best Yaqui is a dead Yaqui" (Hector Aguilar Camín, "The Relevant Tradition: Sonoran Leaders in the Revolution," in D. A. Brading, ed., *Caudillo and Peasant in the Mexican Revolution* [Cambridge: Cambridge University Press, 1980], p. 94).

68. Córdova, *La ideología,* pp. 270–273.

69. Caso, *La comunidad indígena,* pp. 63, 103.

70. Richard Sinkin, *The Mexican Reform, 1855–76: A Study in Liberal Nation-Building* (Austin: University of Texas Press, 1979); Córdova, *La ideología,* pp. 46–62.

71. Caso, *La comunidad indígena,* p. 110.

72. For active *políticos* like Calles, Obregón, or Alvarado, "national reconstruction" was the slogan, to which end Calles preached "a robust nationalism . . . above all; and a firm and energetic resolve to 'make the nation' [*hacer patria*]": (Córdova, *Ideología,* pp. 274, 384). For intellectual variations on this theme, note Krauze, *Caudillos culturales,* pp. 106, 201–202, 212–218, 220–221. Romanell, *Making of the Mexican Mind,* p. 63, concludes that the "cultural rehabilitation" initiated in

1910 by the Ateneo de la Juventud "is the ideological expression of the Mexican Revolution, insofar as we take that Revolution to signify a *discovery* of Mexico *by* Mexicans as well as a *recovery* of Mexico *for* Mexicans."

73. Knight, *Mexican Revolution*, II: 373; Caso, *La comunidad indígena*, pp. 101–102.

74. Brading, *Origins*, pp. 53–54, and idem, *Prophecy and Myth in Mexican History* (Cambridge: Centre for Latin American Studies, 1984), p. 67.

75. Gamio, *Forjando patria*, pp. 5–6, 98.

76. Brading, *Prophecy*, pp. 64–71, offers a succinct and perceptive analysis of Molina Enríquez.

77. Cited by Cabrera, "El balance de la revolución," p. 282.

78. *El Reformador* (founder and editor, Andrés Molina Enríquez), no. 31 (18 September 1936), in AGN/LC 545.3/147.

79. Cabrera, "El balance de la revolución," p. 282.

80. Lind, an ex-governor of Minnesota of Swedish extraction, asserted the superiority not only of the "Teutonic" over the "Latin" races, but also of Mexico's northern mestizo over its southern Indian people; this second judgment was warmly received by racist Carrancistas like Ceballos (*El Demócrata*, 18 January 1916).

81. José Vasconcelos, "The Latin-American Basis of Mexican Civilization," in José Vasconcelos and Manuel Gamio, *Aspects of Mexican Civilization* (Chicago: University of Chicago Press, 1926), pp. 83, 92–94, passim.

82. Gamio, *Forjando patria*, p. 96; Aguirre Beltrán, *Teoría y práctica*, p. 24.

83. Gamio, *Forjando patria*, p. 94.

84. Ibid., pp. 96–97.

85. Simpson, *The Ejido*, pp. 243, 535ff.

86. Caso, *La comunidad indígena*, p. 105, cites the "positive values" of Indian culture which should be protected and conserved during the process of acculturation that he advocates; these include "communal labor, the obligation to perform services [and] respect for natural authorities"—a contentiously normative list!

87. Marvin Harris, quoted by Michael Banton, "The Concept of Racism," in Zubaida, *Race and Racialism*, p. 27.

88. The racist assumptions that underlay high politics are well illustrated in Christopher Thorne, *Allies of a Kind: The United States, Britain and the War against Japan, 1941–1945* (New York: Oxford University Press, 1978), pp. 4–11, 167–168, passim.

89. Reverse racism was apparent not only when conventional hierarchies of "racial" worth were dogmatically reversed, but also—albeit more subtly—when "racial" differences (as against hierarchies) were asserted, often with a view to displaying the distinctive cultural contributions of different "races." "To countenance the concept of race by seeming to show that the great ethnic groups constituting human kind as a whole have, as such, made their own peculiar contributions to our common heritage . . . would simply result in a reversal of racist doctrine. To attribute special psychological characteristics to the biological races,

with a positive definition, is as great a departure from scientific truth as to do so with a negative definition" (Claude Lévi-Strauss, "Race and History," in Leo Kuper, ed., *Race, Science and Society* [New York: Columbia University Press, 1975], p. 95).

90. Gamio, *Forjando patria*, pp. 7–8, 12–13, 21, 24, 94. Writing a decade later, Gamio still retained his racial assumptions: while the "racial characteristics" of the original Mesoamerican native population were "normal," subsequent Indian-Spanish miscegenation, lacking "social, ethical or eugenic tendencies," was "inharmonious" and abnormal, which it remained down to the nineteenth century (when "inter-breeding was still a very abnormal and anti-social thing . . . a convergence of the bad in the two races, not the good"). Furthermore, even today the differences between white and Indian remain "pathologically, anatomically, [and] physiologically . . . extremely great," Gamio, "The Indian Basis of Mexican Civilization," in Vasconcelos and Gamio, *Aspects*, pp. 105, 119, 124. In light of this, as well as of his own evidence, it is difficult to see how David Brading concludes that Gamio was able "to escape from the genetic determinism that then afflicted social thinking in Mexico," "Manuel Gamio," p. 79.

91. Gamio, *Forjando patria*, p. 21.

92. Ibid., p. 23.

93. Vasconcelos, *Aspects,* pp. 84–87, 97. Parallels with Gilberto Freyre's thesis of Luso-Brazilian colonialism spring to mind.

94. Salvador Alvarado, *La reconstrucción de México. Un mensaje a los pueblos de América*, 3 vols. (Mexico: A. Ballesca y Cía., 1919) I: 339, 383–384.

95. Gómez Morín sees Mexico as the "bulwark of the race" against North America; Marte Gómez praises Vasconcelos' grasp of "our racial future"; Múgica invokes "the Aztec blood that . . . generously shed over the centuries . . . in pursuit of the highest ideals, courses hotly before the problems of the race" (Krauze, *Caudillos culturales*, p. 250; idem,*Vida política contemporánea: cartas de Marte R. Gómez*, 2 vols. [Mexico: Fondo de Cultura Económica, 1978)] I: 22; Armando María y Campos, *Múgica: crónica biográfica* [Mexico, Cía. de Ediciones Populares, 1939], pp. 292, 295).

96. Samuel Ramos, *Profile of Man and Culture in Mexico*, transl. Peter G. Earle (1934, reprint, Austin: University of Texas Press, 1975), pp.11, 27, 30–32, 40–41, 63–64, 87, 102, 119–120. Ramos' "Egyptianism'" obviously suggests comparisons with the imputation of "Orientalism" made by Western critics of Islamic society: see Edward W. Said, *Orientalism* (New York: Pantheon Books, 1978).

97. Carlos Marín Foucher, "Iniciativa para crear el servicio militar obligatorio del indio," June 1938, AGN/LC 545.3/147.

98. F. Rodríguez Cano to Departamento de Trabajo, 30 September 1935, AGN/LC 533.4/12.

99. Ramón P. De Negri, "La tragedia biológica y social de nuestros indígenas," n.d. (1938?), AGN/LC 545.3/147.

100. Gamio, *Forjando patria*, pp. 18, 22, 107, 140–141, and idem, *Aspects*, p. 116; Cabrera, "El balance de la revolución," p. 282. Francisco Bulnes' theorized

racial hierarchy, which has been (rightly) seen as a prime example of Porfirian racial thought, stressed the determining factor of food: Francisco Bulnes, *El porvenir de las naciones hispano-americanos ante las recientes conquistas de Europa y Norteamérica* (Mexico: Imprenta de M. Nava, 1899), ch.1; Banton, "The Concept of Racism," p. 25, cites as "the first racist" Robert Knox, the Edinburgh anatomist who "held that each race was adapted to one habitat."

101. Banton, "The Concept of Racism," pp. 17, 31.

102. Rex, "The Concept of Race," pp. 39, 50.

103. Caso, *La comunidad indígena*, p. 93.

104. Gamio, *Forjando patria*, pp. 21, 95.

105. Ramos, *Profile*, pp. 30, 34, 37–40, 56, 119–120. Is it a grotesque misapplication of psychoanalytic theory to equate social collectivities, such as "Mexico," with individuals, thus to infer the existence of a collective unconscious, collective infantile traumas, etc.? I had assumed that such inferences were now generally dismissed by historians and psychoanalysts alike: "The last traces of Freud's notions about the 'racial' mind of inherited collective psychological dispositions that haunted his work have been weeded out by his successors as redundant, almost embarrassing reminders of nineteenth-century superstitions about a 'group soul'": Peter Gay, *Freud for Historians* (New York: Oxford University Press,1985), pp. 146–147; see also David Hackett Fischer, *Historians' Fallacies: Toward a Logic of Historical Thought* (New York: Harper and Row,1970), pp. 192–195. Gay, however, sets out to overturn this consensus, developing—not at all convincingly —"Freud's argument that individual and social psychology are, for all practical purposes, identical," p. 159 and ch. 5, passim.

106. Marroquín, *Balance*, p. 10.

107. Bonfil Batalla, *Utopia*, p. 36; Morin, "Indien, indigenisme, indianité," p. 5 and idem, "Indianité et état," pp. 260, 263.

108. Roger Bartra, "El problema indígena y la ideología indigenista," *Revista Mexicana de Sociología* 36/3 (1974): 462.

109. Such psychological attributions are legitimately seen as deterministic even if they admit some—gradual, generational—transformation: Rex makes the point ("The Concept of Race," pp. 50–51) that "the distinction between deterministic and undeterministic belief systems is not absolute and . . . deterministic assumptions might well be found hidden in a theory of an undeterministic kind. Thus it may be said that a group of people are not yet ready in terms of education or economic advancement to assume equal rights, but if it is also held that the group concerned cannot be expected to advance economically or educationally during 25, 50, or 100 years, the belief operates deterministically." Collective psychological attributions would seem to be even less mutable—and therefore even more strictly deterministic. The empirical arguments against such attributions are many: Friedlander, *Being Indian*, p. 106, makes the telling point that the average illiterate, Nahautl-speaking Hueyapeño "has never heard of Quetzalcoatl, Tlaloc or any other pre-hispanic god"; literacy and education are necessary prerequisites of such cultural

acquisitions.

110. Córdova, *La ideología*, pp. 80–81; Gamio, *Forjando patria*, p. 11. Gamio's views on Protestantism seem to have varied: cf. Brading, "Manuel Gamio," p. 86.

111. Vasconcelos, *Aspects*, pp. 11, 14, and idem, *Memorias, Ulíses criollo, La tormenta* (Mexico: Fondo de Cultura Ecónomica, 1982), p. 6.

112. Aguirre Beltrán, *Obra polémica*, pp. 46–47; Gamio, *Forjando patria*, p. 153.

113. Charles C. Cumberland, "The Sonoran Chinese and the Mexican Revolution," *Hispanic American Historical Review* 40 (1960): 191–211.

114. González Navarro, *La vida social*, pp. 166–172; Cabrera, "El balance de la revolución," p. 281; Evelyn Hu-Dehart, "Immigrants to a Developing Society: The Chinese in Northern Mexico, 1875–1932," *Journal of Arizona History* 21 (1980): 283.

115. Hu-Dehart, "Immigrants," p. 289; Knight, *Mexican Revolution*, I: 207–208.

116. Jesús Garza, Secretary, Comité de Salubridad Pública de San Pedro (Coahuila) Pro-Raza, to President Calles, 3 December 1924, AGN/PEC 104–CH–16.

117. Leo M. D. Jacques, "Have Quick More Money than Mandarins: The Chinese in Sonora," *Journal of Arizona History* 17 (1976): 205.

118. Van den Berghe, *Race and Racism*, pp. 29–30.

119. Hu-Dehart, "Immigrants," pp. 294–295; Jacques, "Chinese in Sonora," pp. 204, 207.

120. Personal communication from William French, on the basis of research done in Parral, Chihuahua.

121. Another relevant parallel suggests itself: the expropriation by nationalist regimes in East Africa of Asian traders and middlemen, who had prospered in symbiosis with colonial business interests, as the Chinese had in symbiosis with the big U.S. companies in Northern Mexico. In both cases, conscious nationalism justified an attack on an "alien" petite bourgeoisie, an attack that promised short-term political and economic advantages to the new nationalist elites (in both cases, too, the symbiotically linked corporate business interests both escaped racist obloquy and weathered economic nationalist pressures pretty well). The East African parallels would include the 1960s policy of Kenyanization and the 1970s expulsion of Asians from Uganda. Both redounded to the benefit of nationalist/ populist regimes; neither affected the basic "dependency" of these economies vis-à-vis multinational capital. Short-term advantage, justified by racist theory, thus made possible a petty nationalization, which was probably economically counter-productive and which occurred in default of any more serious, structural nationalization. In some respects Mexican Sinophobia was, like German anti-Semitism, a "socialism of fools."

122. Alvarado, *La reconstrucción*, I: 148–149.

123. Hu-Dehart, "Immigrants," p. 292.

124. Adolfo Sirateire et al., Cucurpe, Sonora, to President Calles, 14 March 1925, AGN/PEC 104–CH–16, congratulating the president on the "energetic attitude he

has displayed in support of the anti-Chinese campaign".

125. Hugh G. Campbell, *La derecha radical en México, 1929–1949* (Mexico: Sepsetentas, 1976), pp. 51–52, 68, 125, 127. Like its European counterparts, the Mexican secular radical Right of the 1930s combined anti-Semitism with antipathy to Communism and fervent nationalism, a nationalism that, in the Mexican case, claimed "revolutionary" origins (compare Italian fascism) and which built on the traditions of 1920s Sinophobia. More recently, too, Syrio-Lebanese groups have incurred racist attacks, for example, at Juchitán on the Isthmus of Tehuantepec.

126. Caso, *La comunidad indígena*, pp. 109, 155: "Mexican society rejects all racial discrimination"; Cabrera, "El balance de la revolución," p. 281: "In Mexico race prejudices do not, fortunately, exist"; Van den Berghe, *Race and Racism*, p. 55: "The concept of race has become almost totally alien to Mexican culture."

127. Aguirre Beltrán, prologue to Caso, *La comunidad indígena*, p. 39.

128. Brading, *Prophecy and Myth*, p. 71.

129. A 1946 government review of the *indigenista* educational policies of the 1930s and 1940s concluded that "the educational centers [thus established] . . . sustain an effort that is entirely inadequate in the face of the magnitude of the task they face": *México: seis años de actividad nacional* (Mexico: Secretaría de Gobernación, 1946), p. 174. De la Peña, "Orden social," p. 313, concurs.

130. "The departure of heads of families in search of work in the [Chiapas] coffee zone gives a great impulse to the incorporation of the Indian into a civilised state": F. Rodríguez Cabo to Departamento de Trabajo, 30 September 1935, AGN/LC 533.4/12. Studies of migration to the United States frequently make the same point.

131. Seasonal migration has served to channel resources to highland Indian communities in Chiapas or Peru, thus helping to perpetuate both the communities and their "Indian" culture. More recently, the extensive migration of Mixtec workers from Oaxaca to the northern border has resulted in the formation, on the frontier, of a consciously Mixtec community: Michael Kearney, "Mixtec Political Consciousness: From Passive to Active Resistance," paper given at the workshop on "Rural Revolt, the Mexican State and the United States: Historical and Contemporary Views," Center for U.S.-Mexican Studies, University of California, San Diego, February 1986. See also Margarita Nolasco, "Los Indios de México," in Glantz, ed., *Heterodoxia recuperada*, pp. 349–350.

132. Bartra, "El problema indígena," pp. 476–478; Bonfil Batalla, *Utopia y revolución*, pp. 42–43.

133. Redfield, *Folk Culture*, pp. 66–67; see also Rodolfo Stavenhagen, *Las clases sociales en las sociedades agrarias* (Mexico: Siglo Veintiuno, 1971), p. 238.

134. The comments of a cacique in the Valle del Mezquital, quoted in Bartra, "El problema indígena," p. 462.

135. Stavenhagen, "México: minorías étnicas," p. 23. Even before the present spectacular building was erected in the 1960s, its forerunner, the Museo Nacional de Arqueología, Historia y Etnografía, was deemed—by *indigenistas*—to be "the most genuinely national institution of the Republic," a material symbol of ethnic

values and national identity: memorandum of the Organization of the Indians of the Republic to Cárdenas, January 1938, AGN/LC 545.3/147.

136. Friedlander, *Being Indian*, pp. 159–161.

137. Bartra, "El problema indígena," pp. 467, 475.

138. Friedrich, *Princes*, p. 146: "A fundamental issue continued to be whether to ally oneself along the lines of Tarascan Indian ancestry, or in terms of some sort of non-ethnic class."

139. Friedlander, *Being Indian*, p. 71.

140. Friedrich, *Princes*, p. 185.

141. Friedlander, *Being Indian*, p. 30 (though the date of this statement is not clear).

142. Oscar Lewis, *Five Families: Mexican Case Studies in the Culture of Poverty* (London: Souvenir Press, 1976), p. 68.

143. Friedlander, *Being Indian*, pp. 77–79; Vasconcelos, *Aspects*, p. 38.

144. Friedrich, *Princes*, pp. 121, 186.

145. Friedlander, *Being Indian*, pp. xv, 76.

146. P. Beaucage, "Comunidades indígenas de la sierra norte de Puebla," *Revista Mexicana de Sociología* 36 (1974): 144. Other similar examples could be given.

147. Redfield, *Folk Culture*, p. 75; see also Friedlander, *Being Indian*, pp. 72, 148. Barta, "El problema indígena," pp. 461–467.

149. Friedlander, *Being Indian*, p. xvii.

150. Robert Redfield, *Tepoztlán, a Mexican Village* (Chicago: University of Chicago Press, 1946), p. 68.

Bibliography

Ação da bancada paulista "Por São Paulo unido" na Assemblea Constituinte. São Paulo: n.p., 1935, 364–413.

Aguilar Camín, Héctor. *La frontera nómada: Sonora y la Revolución Mexicana.* Mexico: Siglo Veintiuno, 1985.

————. "The Relevant Tradition: Sonoran Leaders in the Revolution." In D. A. Brading, ed., *Caudillo and Peasant in the Mexican Revolution.* Cambridge: Cambridge University Press, 1980.

Aguirre, Sergio. "El cincuentenario de un gran crimen." *Cuba Socialista* 2, 16 (December 1962): 33–51.

Aguirre Beltrán, Gonzalo. "The Indian and the Mexican Revolution." Mimeo, Benson Latin American Collection, University of Texas at Austin.

————. *Obra polémica.* Mexico: Instituto Nacional de Antropología e Historia, 1976.

————. *La población negra de México, 1519–1810.* Mexico: Ediciones Fuente Cultural, 1946.

————. "Prólogo." In Alfonso Caso, *La comunidad indígena.* Mexico: Secretaría de Educación Pública, 1971, 7–41.

————. *Teoría y práctica de la educación indígena.* Mexico: Sepsetentas, 1973.

Alatas, Syed Hussein. *The Myth of the Lazy Native.* London: Frank Cass, 1977.

Alberdi, Juan Bautista. *Bases y puntos de partida para la organización política de la confederación argentina.* 1852. Reprint. Buenos Aires: Editorial Plus Ultra, 1981.

Alfonso, Ramón M. *La prostitución en Cuba y especialmente en La Habana.* Havana: Imprenta P. Fernández y Cía., 1902.

Almeida, Fernando H. Mendes de. *Constituições do Brasil.* São Paulo: Saraiva, 1963.

Altman, Ida, and James Lockhart, eds. *Provinces of Early Mexico: Variants of Spanish American Regional Evolution.* Berkeley & Los Angeles: University of California Press, 1976.

Alvarado, Salvador. *La reconstrucción de México. Un mensaje a los pueblos de América.* Mexico: A. Ballesca y Cía., 3 vols., 1919.

Alvarez Suárez, Augustín E. *La herencia moral de los pueblos hispano-americanos.* Buenos Aires: Casa Vaccaro, 1919.

————. *La transformación de las razas en América.* Barcelona: F. Granada, 1906.

————. *South America: ensayo de psicología política.* 1894. Reprint. Buenos Aires: "La Cultura Argentina," 1918.

Alves, Henrique L. *Nina Rodrigues e o Negro do Brasil.* São Paulo: Asociação Cultural do

Negro, [1962].

Anais da Câmara dos Deputados, 1921. Rio de Janeiro: n.p., 1923.

Andrade, Mário de. "O samba rural Paulista." *Revista do Arquivo Municipal* 41 (November 1937): 37–116.

Andrews, George Reid. *The Afro-Argentines of Buenos Aires, 1800–1900*. Madison: University of Wisconsin Press, 1980.

————. "Black Workers and White: São Paulo, Brazil, 1888–1928." *Hispanic American Historical Review* 50, 3 (August 1988): 491–524.

Archivo Nacional de Cuba, Fondo de la Audiencia de La Habana, Causa 321/1910 contra el Partido Independiente de Color, Leg. 228-1, 229-1, 529-1, 520-4.

Armas, Rogelio de. "Nuestra población rural y la Liga agraria." *Cuba Contemporánea* 4 (January 1914): 74–87.

Avni, Haim. *Argentina y la historia de la inmigración judía, 1810–1950*. Buenos Aires & Jerusalem: Editorial Universitaria Magnes-AMIA, 1986.

Ayarragaray, Lucas. *La anarquía argentina y el caudillismo, estudio psicológico de los orígenes argentinos*. 2d ed. Buenos Aires: J. Lajouane y Cía. Editores, 1925.

————. "La mestización de las razas en América y sus consecuencias degenerativas." *Revista de Filosofía, Cultura, Ciencias, Educación* 3 (Buenos Aires, 1st sem. 1916): 21–41.

Azevedo, Fernando de. *Brazilian Culture: An Introduction to the Study of Culture in Brazil.* Translated by William Rex Crawford. New York: Macmillan, 1950.

Baily, Samuel L. "Marriage Patterns and Immigrant Assimilation in Buenos Aires, 1882–1923." *Hispanic American Historical Review* 60, no. 1 (February 1980): 32–48.

Banton, Michael. "The Concept of Racism." In Sami Zubaida, ed., *Race and Racialism*. London: Tavistock, 1970, 17–34.

————. *Racial Theories*. Cambridge, England: Cambridge University Press, 1987.

Barre, Marie-Chantal. *Ideologías indigenistas y movimientos indios*. Mexico: Siglo Veintiuno, 1983.

Barros, Roque Spencer Maciel de. *A ilustração brasileira e a idéia de universidade*. São Paulo: Universidade de São Paulo, 1959.

Barroso, Gustavo. *O que o integralista deve saber*. Rio de Janeiro: Civilização Brasileira, 1935.

Bartra, Roger. "El problema indígena y la ideología indigenista." *Revista Mexicana de Sociología* 36/3 (1974): 459–482.

Bataillon, Claude. "Note sur l'indigénisme au Mexique." In *Indianité, ethnocide, indigénisme en Amérique Latine*. Paris: Editions du Centre National de la Recherche Scientifique, 1982.

Beaucage, Pierre. "Comunidades indígenas de la sierra norte de Puebla." *Revista Mexicana de Sociología* 36 (1974): 111–147.

Belo, José Maria. *Ensaios políticos e literários: Ruy Barbosa e escritos diversos*. Rio de Janeiro: Castilho, 1918.

Benjamin, Thomas L. "Passages to Leviathan: Chiapas and the Mexican State, 1891–1947." PhD diss., Michigan State University, 1981.

Blackwelder, Julia Kirk, and Lyman L. Johnson. "Changing Criminal Patterns in Buenos Aires, 1890 to 1914." *Journal of Latin American Studies* 14, no. 2 (November 1982): 359–380.

Bomilcar, Alvaro. *A política no Brasil ou o nacionalismo radical*. Rio de Janeiro: Leite

Ribeiro, 1920.

———. *O preconceito de raça no Brasil.* Rio de Janeiro: Aurora, 1916.

Bonfil Batalla, Guillermo. *Utopia y revolución: El pensamiento político contemporáneo de los indios en América Latina.* Mexico: Editorial Nueva Imagen, 1981.

Brading, David. "Manuel Gamio and Official Indigenismo in Mexico." *Bulletin of Latin American Research* 7 (1988): 75–89.

———. *The Origins of Mexican Nationalism.* Cambridge: Centre of Latin American Studies, 1985.

———. *Prophecy and Myth in Mexican History.* Cambridge: Centre for Latin American Studies, 1984.

Braga, Osvaldo Melo, ed. *Bibliografia de Joaquim Nabuco.* Instituto Nacional do Livro, Coleção Bl. Bibliografia 8. Rio de Janeiro: Imprensa Nacional, 1952.

Bruno, Cayetano. *Los salesianos y las hijas de María Auxiliadora en la Argentina.* Buenos Aires: Instituto Salesiano de Artes Gráficas, 1981.

Bryce, James. *South America: Observations and Impressions.* New York: Macmillan, 1912.

Bulnes, Francisco. *El porvenir de las naciones hispano-americanos ante las recientes conquistas de Europa y Norteamérica.* Mexico: Imprenta de M. Nava, 1899.

Bunge, Carlos Octavio. *Nuestra América (Ensayo de psicología social).* 1903. Reprint. Buenos Aires: Casa Vaccaro, 1918.

———. *Nuestra patria. Libro de lectura para la educación nacional.* Buenos Aires: A. Estrada y Cía. Editores, (1910?).

Burns, E. Bradford. *The Poverty of Progress: Latin America in the Nineteenth Century.* Berkeley & Los Angeles: University of California Press, 1980.

Cabrera, Luis. "El balance de la revolución." In *La revolución es la revolución.* Guanajuato: Ediciones del Gobierno del Estado de Guanajuato, 1977, 255–298.

Cabrera, Raimundo. *Cuba y sus jueces: rectificaciones oportunas.* Havana: Imprenta "El Retiro," 1887.

———. "Llamamiento a los cubanos por la Sociedad Económica de Amigos del País." *Revista Bimestre Cubana* 18, no. 2 (March–April 1923): 81–84.

Campbell, Hugh G. *La derecha radical en México, 1929–1949.* Mexico: Sepsetentas, 1976.

Carbonell, Walterio. *Crítica. Cómo surgio la cultura nacional.* Havana: Editorial Yaka, 1961.

Carneiro, Edison. *Ladinos e crioulos.* Rio de Janeiro: Civilização Brasileira, 1964.

———. *Religiões negras.* Rio de Janeiro: Civilização Brasileira, 1936.

Carneiro, Maria Luiza Tucci. *O anti-semitismo na era Vargas.* São Paulo: Brasiliense, 1988.

Carrera y Justiz, Francisco. *El municipio y la cuestión de razas.* Havana: Imprenta la Moderna Poesía, 1904.

———. *El municipio y los extranjeros. Los españoles en Cuba.* Havana: Imprenta la Moderna Poesía, 1904.

Carrión, Miguel de. "El desenvolvimiento social de Cuba en los últimos veinte años." *Revista Bimestre Cubana* 18, no. 4 (July–August 1923): 313–319, and 18, no. 5 (September–October 1923): 345–364.

Chang, Frederico. *El ejército nacional en la república neocolonial, 1899–1933.* Havana: Editorial de Ciencias Sociales, 1981.

Conrad, Robert. *The Destruction of Brazilian Slavery, 1850–1888.* Berkeley: University of California Press, 1972.

Conte, Rafael, and José M. Capmany. *Guerra de razas (negros contra blancos en Cuba).*

Havana: Imprenta Militar Antonio Pérez, 1912.

Copello, Santiago Luis. *Gestiones del arzobispo Aneiros en favor de los indios hasta la conquista del desierto.* Buenos Aires: Imprenta "Coni," 1945.

Córdova, Arnaldo. *La ideologia de la revolución mexicana: la formación del nuevo régimen.* Mexico: Ediciones Era, 1973.

Costa, Emília. Viotti da. *The Brazilian Empire: Myths and Histories.* Chicago: University of Chicago Press, 1985.

Costa, João Cruz. *Contribuição à história das idéias no Brasil.* Rio de Janeiro: José Olympio, 1956.

Costa, Octavio R. *Juan Gualberto Gómez, una vida sin sombra.* Havana: Editorial Unidad, 1950.

Crawford, William Rex. *A Century of Latin American Thought.* Cambridge, Mass.: Harvard University Press, 1961.

Cruz, Manuel de la. *La revolución cubana y la raza de color (apuntes y datos) por un cubano sin odios.* Key West, Fla.: Imprenta "La Propaganda," 1895.

Cumberland, Charles C. "The Sonoran Chinese and the Mexican Revolution." *Hispanic American Historical Review* 40 (1960): 191–211.

Cunha, Euclides da. *Os sertões.* 2d ed. Rio de Janeiro: Laemmert, 1903.

———. *Rebellion in the Backlands.* Chicago: University of Chicago Press, 1944.

Degler, Carl N. *Neither Black nor White.* New York: Macmillan, 1971.

De la Peña, Guillermo. "Orden social y educación indígena en México: la pervivencia de un legado colonial." In Susana Glantz, ed., *La heterodoxia recuperada: en torno a Angel Palerm.* Mexico: Fondo de Cultura Ecónomica, 1987.

Diario de la Marina, El (Havana), esp. 1910.

Diario de los debates del congreso constituyente, 1916–1917. Mexico: Talleres Gráficos de la Nación, 2 vols., 1960.

Diegues Júnior, Manuel. *Imigração, urbanização e industrialização.* Rio de Janeiro: Centro Brasileiro de Pesquisas Educacionais, 1961.

Dirección política de las F.A.R., ed. *Historia de Cuba.* 1967. Reprint. Havana: Instituto Cubano del Libro, 1971.

Directorio Central de la Raza de Color. *Reglamento del Directorio Central de la Raza de Color.* Havana: Imprenta la Lucha, 1892.

Duke, Cathy. "The Idea of Race: The Cultural Impact of American Intervention in Cuba, 1898–1912." In Blanca G. Silvestrini, ed., *Politics, Society and Culture in the Caribbean. Selected Papers of the XIV Conference of Caribbean Historians,* pp. 87–109. San Juan: Universidad de Puerto Rico, 1983.

Elkin, Judith Laikin. *Jews of Latin American Republics.* Chapel Hill: University of North Carolina Press, 1980.

Fabela, Isidro. *Documentos históricos de la revolución mexicana, revolución y régimen constitucionalista.* Mexico: Fondo de Cultura Ecónomica, 27 vols., 1960–1973.

Fermoselle, Rafael. *Política y color en Cuba. La Guerrita de 1912.* Montevideo: Editorial Geminis, 1974.

Fernández Robaina, Tomás. *Bibliografía de temas afrocubanos.* Havana: Biblioteca Nacional "José Martí," 1985.

———. "El negro en Cuba, 1902–1958. Apuntes para la historia de la lucha contra la discriminación racial en la neocolonia." Unpublished paper.

Figueras, Francisco. *Cuba y su evolución colonial.* Havana: Imprenta Avisador Comercial,

1907.

―――. *La intervención y su política.* Havana: Imprenta Avisador Comercial, 1906.

―――. *Rio Branco e Euclides da Cunha.* Rio de Janeiro: Ministerio das Relações Exteriores, 1946.

Fischer, David Hackett. *Historians' Fallacies: Toward a Logic of Historical Thought.* New York: Harper & Row, 1970.

Foner, Philip S. *The Spanish-Cuban-American War and the Birth of American Imperialism, 1895–1902.* 2 vols. New York: Monthly Review Press, 1972.

Fontaine, Pierre-Michel, ed. *Race, Class and Power in Brazil.* Los Angeles: Center for Latin American Studies, UCLA, 1985.

Fredrickson, George M. *The Black Image in the White Mind: The Debate on Afro-American Character and Destiny, 1817–1914.* 2d ed. Middletown, Conn.: Wesleyan University Press, 1987.

Freyre, Gilberto. *Atualidade de Euclides da Cunha.* Rio de Janeiro: Casa do Estudante do Brasil, 1964.

―――. *Casa grande e senzala.* Rio de Janeiro: José Olympio, 1933.

―――. *The Masters and the Slaves.* 2d ed. Translated by Samuel Putnam. New York: Knopf, 1956.

―――. *O mundo que o Português criou.* Rio de Janeiro: José Olympio, 1940.

―――. *Ordem e progresso.* Rio de Janeiro: José Olympio, 1959.

―――. *Sobrados e mucambos.* São Paulo: José Olympio, 1936. (Published in English as *The Mansions and the Shanties.* Translated and edited by Harriet de Onís. New York: Knopf, 1963.)

Friedlander, Judith. *Being Indian in Hueyapan: A Study of Forced Identity in Contemporary Mexico.* New York: St. Martin's Press, 1975.

Friedrich, Paul. *The Princes of Naranja: An Essay in Anthrohistorical Method.* Austin: University of Texas Press, 1986.

Gallo, Ezequiel. *Farmers in Revolt: The Revolution of 1893 in the Province of Santa Fé, Argentina.* London: Athlone Press, 1976.

Gamio, Manuel. *Forjando patria.* Mexico: Editorial Porrúa, 1960.

García, Juan Agustín. *La ciudad indiana (Buenos Aires desde 1600 hasta mediados del siglo XVIII).* Buenos Aires: A. Estrada y Cía., 1900.

Gay, Peter. *Freud for Historians.* New York: Oxford University Press, 1985.

Glick, Thomas F., ed. *The Comparative Reception of Darwinism.* Austin: University of Texas Press, 1974.

Glickman, Nora. "The Image of the Jew in Brazilian and Argentinian Literature." PhD diss., New York University, 1978.

Gómez, Marte R. *Vida política contemporánea: cartas de Marte R. Gómez.* 2 vols. Mexico: Fondo de Cultura Ecónomica, 1978.

González, Joaquín V. *Obras completas,* 25 vols. Buenos Aires: Imprenta Mercatali, 1935–1937.

González, Luis. *Historia de la revolución mexicana, 1934–40. Los días del presidente Cárdenas.* Mexico: El Colegio de México, 1981.

González Navarro, Moisés. *Historia moderna de México: El Porfiriato, la vida social.* Mexico: Editorial Hermes, 1970.

―――. "*Mestizaje* in Mexico during the National Period." In Magnus Mörner, ed., *Race and Class in Latin America.* New York: Columbia University Press, 1971, 145–155.

Gould, Stephen Jay. *Ever Since Darwin: Reflections in Natural History.* Harmondsworth:

Penguin Books, 1986. (Originally published, New York: Norton, 1977.)

Gouvea Filho, Pedro. *E. Roquette-Pinto: o antropólogo e educador*. Rio de Janeiro: Ministério da Educação e Cultura, Instituto Nacional de Cinema Educativo, 1955.

Graham, Loren R. "Science and Values: The Eugenics Movement in Germany and Russia in the 1920s." *American Historical Review* 82, no. 5 (December 1977): 1113–1164.

Graham, Richard. *Britain and the Onset of Modernization in Brazil, 1850–1914*. Cambridge: Cambridge University Press, 1968.

Guerra, François-Xavier. *De l'Ancien Régime à la Révolution*. 2 vols. Paris, Editions L'Harmattan, 1985.

Guerra y Sánchez, Ramiro. *Un cuarto de siglo de evolución cubana*. Havana: Librería "Cervantes," 1924.

Guillaumin, Colette. *L'idéologie raciste. Genèse et langage actuel*. Paris: Mouton, 1972.

Guiral Moreno, Mario. "Nuestros problemas políticos, económicos y sociales." *Cuba Contemporánea* 5 (August 1914): 401–424.

Guiteras, Juan. "Estudios demográficos. Aclimatación de la raza blanca en los trópicos." *Revista Bimestre Cubana* 8, no. 2 (November–December 1913): 405–421.

———. "Patología médica. La fiebre amarilla considerada como enfermedad de la infancia en los focos antillanos." In *La ciencia en Cuba. Recopilación por José Manuel Carbonell y Rivero*. Havana: Imprenta Montalvo y Cárdenas, 1928, 217–226.

Haberly, David T. *Three Sad Races: Racial Identity and National Consciousness in Brazilian Literature*. Cambridge: Cambridge University Press, 1983.

Haller, John S., Jr. *Outcasts from Evolution: Scientific Attitudes of Racial Inferiority, 1859–1900*. Urbana: University of Illinois Press, 1971.

Halperín Donghi, Tulio. "Para qué la inmigración? Ideología y política inmigratoria en la Argentina (1810–1914)." In Tulio Halperín Donghi, *El espejo de la historia. Problemas argentinos y perspectivas hispanoamericanas*. Buenos Aires: Editorial Sudamericana, 1987, 189–238.

Hanke, Lewis. *Aristotle and the American Indians: A Study in Race Prejudice in the Modern World*. London: Hollis & Carter, 1959.

Harris, Marvin. *Patterns of Race in the Americas*. New York: Walker, 1964.

Hasenbalg, Carlos A. *Discriminação e desigualdades raciais no Brasil*. Rio de Janeiro: Graal, 1979.

———. *Race Relations in Modern Brazil*. Albuquerque: Latin American Institute, University of New Mexico, n.d.

Helg, Aline. "The Idea of Race in Argentina, 1880–1930." Unpublished paper, 1987.

Hell, Jurgen. "Das 'sudbrasilianische Neudeutschland': Der annexionistische Grundzug der wilhelmnischen und nazistischen Brasilienpolitik, 1895–1943." In *Der Deutsche Faschismus in Lateinamerika, 1933–1943*. Berlin: n.p., 1966, 103–124.

Hernández Díaz, Jorge. "Relaciones interétnicas contemporáneas en Oaxaca." In Alicia M. Barabas and Miguel A. Bartolomé, eds., *Etnicidad y pluralismo cultural: La dinámica étnica en Oaxaca*. Mexico: Instituto Nacional de Antropología e Historia, 1986, 299–329.

"Histórico e Instrucções para a Execução do Recenseamento de 1920." *Recenseamento do Brazil realizado em 1 de Setembro 1920* 1: 488–489.

Hoernel, Robert B. "Sugar and Social Change in Oriente, Cuba, 1898–1946." *Journal of Latin American Studies* 8, no. 2 (November 1976): 215–249.

Hofstadter, Richard. *Social Darwinism in American Thought, 1860–1915*. Philadelphia: University of Pennsylvania Press, 1944.

Horrego Estuch, Leopoldo. "El alzamiento del doce." *Bohemia* 59, no. 25 (23 June 1967): 18–22.

———. *Juan Gualberto Gómez, un gran inconforme.* Havana: Editorial Mecenas, 1949.

Hu-Dehart, Evelyn. "Immigrants to a Developing Society: The Chinese in Northern Mexico, 1875–1932." *Journal of Arizona History* 21 (1980): 275–312.

Ingenieros, José. *Crónicas de viaje, 1905–1906.* 1908. Reprint. Buenos Aires: R. J. Roggero & Cía., 1951.

———. "La formación de una raza argentina." *Revista de Filosofía, Cultura, Ciencias, Educación* 2 (2nd sem. 1915): 464–483.

———. *La locura en Argentina; locura y brujería en la sociedad colonial, los antiguos "loqueros" de Buenos Aires, los alienados durante la revolución, los alienados en la época de Rosas, los estudios psiquiátricos en la Argentina, los modernos asilos para alienados, censo aproximativo de alienados.* 1920. Reprint. Buenos Aires: Cooperativa Editora Limitada, 1937.

———. *Simulación de la locura ante la sociología criminal y la clínica psiquiátrica.* Buenos Aires: Editorial "La Semana Médica," 1903.

———. *Sociología argentina.* 1910. Reprint. Madrid: D. Jorro, Editor, 1913.

Instituto Brasileiro de Geografia e Estatística. *O Brasil em números.* Rio de Janeiro: IBGE, 1966.

Jacques, Leo M. "Have Quick More Money than Mandarins: The Chinese in Sonora." *Journal of Arizona History* 17 (1976): 201–218.

Jordan, Winthrop P. *White over Black: American Attitudes toward the Negro, 1550–1812.* 1968. Reprint New York: Norton, 1977.

Jorrín, Miguel, and John D. Martz. *Latin American Political Thought and Ideology.* Chapel Hill: University of North Carolina Press, 1970.

Joseph, Gilbert M. *Revolution from Without: Yucatán, Mexico and the United States, 1880–1924.* Cambridge: Cambridge University Press, 1982.

Katz, Friedrich, ed. *Porfirio Díaz frente al descontento popular regional, 1891–1893.* Mexico: Universidad Iberoamericana, 1986.

Kearney, Michael. "Mixtec Political Consciousness: From Passive to Active Resistance." In Daniel Nugent, ed., *Rural Revolt in Mexico and U.S. Intervention.* San Diego: Center for U.S.-Mexican Studies, 1988, 113–124.

Kiple, Kenneth F. *Blacks in Colonial Cuba, 1774–1899.* Gainesville: University Presses of Florida, 1976.

Knight, Alan. "Mexican Peonage: What Was It and Why Was It?" *Journal of Latin American Studies* 18 (1986): 41–74.

———. *The Mexican Revolution.* 2 vols. Cambridge: Cambridge University Press, 1986.

Koster, Henry. *Travels in Brazil.* London: Longman, 1816.

Krauze, Enrique. *Caudillos culturales en la revolución mexicana.* Mexico: Siglo Veintiuno, 1976.

———. *Porfirio Díaz.* Mexico: Fondo de Cultura Económica, 1987.

Leão, A. Carneiro, et al. *À margem da história da República.* Rio de Janeiro: Annuario do Brasil, 1924.

Le Bon, Gustave. *Les lois psychologiques de l'évolution des peuples.* 1894. Reprint. Paris: F. Alcan, 1927.

Le Riverend, Julio. *La república. Dependencia y revolución.* 4th ed. rev. Havana: Instituto Cubano del Libro, 1975.

Levine, Robert M. *The Vargas Regime: The Critical Years, 1934–1938*. New York: Columbia University Press, 1970.

Lévi-Strauss, Claude. "Race and History." In Leo Kuper, ed., *Race, Science and Society*. New York: Columbia University Press, 1975, 95–134.

Lewis, Oscar. *Five Families: Mexican Case Studies in the Culture of Poverty*. London: Souvenir Press, 1976.

———. *Pedro Martínez: A Mexican Peasant and His Family*. London: Panther Books, 1969.

Lima, Alceu Amoroso. *Estudos literários*. 2 vols. Rio de Janeiro: Aguilar, 1966.

Lins, Alvaro. *Ensaio sobre Roquette-Pinto e a ciência como literatura*. Rio de Janeiro: Ed. de Ouro, 1967.

Lins e Silva, Augusto. *Atualidade de Nina Rodrigues*. Rio de Janeiro: Leitura, 1945.

Livingstone, Frank B. "On the non-existence of human races." In Ashley Montagu, ed., *The Concept of Race*. New York: Free Press of Glencoe, 1964, 46–60.

Lombardo Toledano, Vicente. *El problema del indio*. Mexico: Secretaría de Educación Pública, 1973.

Lowenstein, Karl. *Brazil under Vargas*. New York: Macmillan, 1942.

María y Campos, Armando. *Múgica: crónica biográfica*. Mexico: Cía. de Ediciones Populares, 1939.

Marino Flores, Anselmo. "Indian Population and Its Identification." In Manning Nash, ed., *Handbook of Middle American Indians* 6: *Social Anthropology*. Austin: University of Texas Press, 1975.

Marroquín, Alejandro. *Balance del indigenismo. Informe sobre la política indígena en América Latina*. Mexico: Instituto Indigenista Interamericano, 1972.

Martí, José. *Obras completas*. 28 vols. Havana: Editorial Nacional de Cuba, 1963–1973.

Martinez-Alier, Verena. *Marriage, Class and Colour in Nineteenth-Century Cuba. A Study of Racial Attitude and Sexual Values in a Slave Society*. London: Cambridge University Press, 1974.

Masferrer, Marianne, and Carmelo Mesa-Lago. "The Gradual Integration of the Black in Cuba: Under the Colony, the Republic, and the Revolution." In Robert B. Toplin, ed., *Slavery and Race Relations in Latin America*. Westport & London: Greenwood Press, 1974, 348–384.

Meade, Teresa, and Gregory Alonso Pirio. "In Search of the Afro-American 'Eldorado': Attempts by North American Blacks to Enter Brazil in the 1920s." *Luso-Brazilian Review* 25, no. 1 (Summer 1988): 85–110.

Méndez Capote, Renée. *Memorias de una cubanita que nació con el siglo*. 1964. Reprint. Havana: Instituto Cubano del Libro, 1976.

México: seis años de actividad nacional. Mexico: Secretaría de Gobernación, 1946.

Molina Enríquez, Andrés. *Los grandes problemas nacionales*. Mexico: A. Carranza, 1909.

Monitor de la educación común, El (Buenos Aires).

Montagu, [M. F.] Ashley. *The Idea of Race*. Lincoln: University of Nebraska Press, 1965.

———. *Man's Most Dangerous Myth*. New York: Columbia University Press, 1942.

———. *Race, Science and Humanity*. New York: Van Nostrand Reinhold, 1963.

Montalvo, J. R., C. de la Torre, and L. Montané. *El cráneo de Antonio Maceo (Estudio antropológico)*. Havana: Imprenta Militar, 1900.

Morin, Françoise. "Indien, indigenisme, indianité." In *Indianité, ethnocide, indigenisme en Amérique Latine*. Paris: Editions du Centre National de la Recherche Scientifique, 1982, 3–10.

Morro, Juan del (Fernando Ortiz). "La Sociedad de Folklore Cubano." *Revista Bimestre Cubana* 18, no. 1 (January–February 1923): 47–52.

Morúa Delgado, Martín. *Obras completas.* 6 vols. Havana: Edición de la Comisión Nacional del Centenario de Martín Morúa Delgado, 1957.

Moura, Clovis. *Introdução ao pensamento de Euclides da Cunha.* Rio de Janeiro: Civilização Brasileira, 1964.

Mustelier, Gustavo Enrique. *La extinción del negro. Apuntes político-sociales.* Havana: Impr. de Rambla, Bouza y Ca., 1912.

Nabuco, Joaquim. *O abolicionismo.* London: Abraham Kingdon, 1883. (Published in English as *Abolitionism: The Brazilian Antislavery Struggle.* Translated and edited by Robert Conrad. Urbana: University of Illinois Press, 1977.)

———. *Obras completas.* Vol. 11, *Discursos parlamentares 1879–1889.* São Paulo: Instituto Progresso, 1949.

Needell, Jeffrey. *A Tropical Belle Epoque.* Cambridge: Cambridge University Press, 1987.

Neiva, Arthur. *Daqui e de longe: chrônicas nacionais e de viagem.* São Paulo: Melhoramentos, [1927].

Newby, I. A. *Jim Crow's Defense: Anti-Negro Thought in America, 1900–1930.* Baton Rouge: Louisiana State University Press, 1965.

Newton, Ronald C. *German Buenos Aires, 1900–1933: Social Change and Cultural Crisis.* Austin: University of Texas Press, 1977.

Nolasco, Margarita. "Los Indios de México." In Susana Glantz, ed., *La heterodoxia recuperada: en torno a Angel Palerm.* Mexico: Fondo de Cultura Ecónomica, 1987, 347–367.

Nuttini, Hugo G., and Betty Bell. *Ritual Kinship: The Structure and Historical Development of the Compadrazgo System in Rural Tlaxcala.* 2 vols. Princeton: Princeton University Press, 1980.

Ortiz, Fernando. *La crisis política (sus causas y remedios).* Havana: Imprenta y Papelería "La Universal," 1919.

———. "La decadencia cubana: conferencia de renovación patriótica." *Revista Bimestre Cubana* 47 (January–February 1924): 17–44.

———. *Entre cubanos.* 1914(?). Reprint. Havana: Editorial de Ciencias Sociales, 1987.

———. *Hampa afrocubana. Los negros brujos (apuntes para un estudio de etnología criminal).* 1906. Reprint. Madrid: Editorial América, (1917?).

———. *Hampa afrocubana. Los negros esclavos.* 1916. Reprint. Havana: Editorial de Ciencias Sociales, 1975.

———. *La reconquista de América.* Paris: P. Ollendorff, 1911.

Orum, Thomas T. "The Politics of Color: The Racial Dimension of Cuban Politics during the Early Republican Years, 1900–1912." PhD diss., New York University, 1975.

Patrocínio, José do. Editorial in *Gazeta da Tarde*, May 5, 1887. (Reprinted in Afonso Celso, *Oito anos de Parlamento, poder pessoal de D. Pedro II*, São Paulo: Melhoramentos, [1928], 131–132.)

Paz, Octavio. *The Other Mexico: Critique of the Pyramid.* Translated by Lysander Kemp. New York: Grove Press, 1972.

Pereira, Gonçalo de Athayde. *Prof. Manuel Querino: sua vida e suas obras.* Bahia: Imprensa Oficial do Estado, 1932.

Pérez, Louis A., Jr. *Cuba under the Platt Amendment, 1902–1934.* Pittsburgh: University of Pittsburgh Press, 1986.

————. "Politics, Peasants, and People of Color: The 1912 'Race War' in Cuba Reconsidered." *Hispanic American Historical Review* 66, no. 3 (August 1986): 509–539.

Pérez, Pelayo. "El peligro amarillo y el peligro negro." *Cuba Contemporánea* 9 (November 1915): 251–259.

Pérez de la Riva, Juan. "Los recursos humanos de Cuba al comenzar el siglo: inmigración, economía y nacionalidad (1899–1906)." In *La república neocolonial. Anuario de estudios cubanos* 1. Havana: Editorial de Ciencias Sociales, 1975, 7–44.

Pichardo, Hortensia. *Documentos para la historia de Cuba.* 5 vols. Havana: Editorial de Ciencias Sociales, 1968–1980.

Portuondo Linares, Serafín. *Los Independientes de Color. Historia del Partido Independiente de Color.* Havana: Publicaciones del Ministerio de Educación, 1950.

Powell, T. G. "Mexican Intellectuals and the Indian Question, 1876–1911." *Hispanic American Historical Review* 48 (1968): 19–36.

Prazeres, Otto. "Aspectos do Rio Branco." *Revista do Instituto Histórico e Geográfico Brasileiro* 244 (July–September 1959): 343–345.

Primelles, León. *Crónica cubana 1915–1918. La reelección de Menocal y la revolución de 1917. La danza de los millones. La primera guerra mundial.* Havana: Editorial Lex, 1955.

————. *Crónica cubana 1919–1922. Menocal y la Liga nacional. Zayas y Crowder. Fin de la danza de los millones y reajuste.* Havana: Editorial Lex, 1957.

Pueblo, El (Buenos Aires), esp. 1910, 1918.

Putnam, Samuel. "Brazilian Literature." In *Handbook of Latin American Studies* V. Gainesville: University of Florida Press, 1939, 357.

Querino, Manoel. *The African Contribution to Brazilian Civilization.* Translated by E. Bradford Burns. Tempe: Center for Latin American Studies, Arizona State University, 1978.

————. *Costumes africanos no Brasil.* Rio de Janeiro: Civilização Brasileira, 1938.

Raat, William D. "Ideas and Society in Don Porfirio's Mexico." *The Americas* 30 (1973): 32–53.

Ramos, Artur. *As culturas negras no mundo novo.* Rio de Janeiro: Civilização Brasileira, 1937.

————. *O folk-lore negro do Brasil.* Rio de Janeiro: Civilização Brasileira, 1935.

————. *O negro na civilização brasileira.* Rio de Janeiro: Casa do Estudante do Brasil, 1956.

Ramos, Guerreiro. *Guerra e relações de raça.* Rio de Janeiro: União Brasileira de Estudantes, 1943.

————. *Introdução crítica à sociologia brasileira.* Rio de Janeiro: Andes, 1957.

Ramos, José Antonio. *Entreactos.* Havana: R. Veloso Editores, 1913.

Ramos, Samuel. *Profile of Man and Culture in Mexico.* Translated by Peter G. Earle. Austin: University of Texas Press, 1975.

Ramos Mejía, José María. *Las multitudes argentinas. Estudio de psicología colectiva para servir de introducción al libro "Rosas y su tiempo."* 1899. Reprint. Buenos Aires: F. Lajouane, and Madrid: V. Suárez, 1912.

Rebouças, André Pinto. *Agricultura nacional: estudos econômicos.* Rio de Janeiro: Lamoureux, 1883.

Reck, Gregory G. *In the Shadow of Tlaloc: Life in a Mexican Village.* Harmondsworth: Penguin Books, 1978.

Redfield, Robert. *Tepoztlán, a Mexican Village.* Chicago: University of Chicago Press, 1946.

————. *The Folk Culture of Yucatan.* Chicago: University of Chicago Press, 1950.

República Argentina. Congreso Nacional. *Diario de sesiones de la cámara de diputados, año 1879.* Buenos Aires: "La República," 1879.

————. Congreso Nacional. *Diario de sesiones de la cámara de diputados, año 1882.* Buenos Aires: Imprenta de "El Courrier de La Plata." 1882.

————. Congreso Nacional. *Diario de sesiones de la cámara de diputados, año 1884.* Buenos Aires: Imprenta Stiller y Laas, 1884.

República de Cuba. Colección legislativa. *Vol. 21: Leyes, decretos y resoluciones de 1° de julio a 31 de diciembre de 1906.* Havana: Impr. y Papelería de Rambla y Bouza, 1911.

————. Secretaría de Estado (Documentos diplomáticos). *Copia de la correspondencia cambiada entre la legación de su Majestad británica en la Habana y la Secretaría de Estado de la República, relativa al trato de los inmigrantes jamaiquinos.* Havana: n.p., 1924.

Rex, John. "The Concept of Race in Sociological Theory." In Sami Zubaida, ed., *Race and Racialism.* London: Tavistock, 1970, 35–55.

Rio, João do [João Paulo Coelho Barreto]. *As religiões no Rio.* Rio de Janeiro: Garnier, 1906.

Risquet, Juan F. *La cuestión político-social en la isla de Cuba.* Havana: Tipografía "América," 1900.

Rodrigues, A. Coelho. *Manual do subdito fiel ou cartas de um lavrador a Sua Majestade o Imperador sobre a questão do elemento servil.* Rio de Janeiro: Moreira Maximo, 1884.

Rodrigues, José Honório. *Brazil and Africa.* Berkeley: University of California Press, 1965.

Rodrigues, Raimundo Nina. *Os Africanos no Brasil.* 3d ed. São Paulo: Ed. Nacional, 1945.

Rojas, Ricardo. *Blasón de Plata: meditaciones y evocaciones sobre el abolengo de los argentinos.* Buenos Aires: M. García, 1912.

————. *Eurindía: ensayo de estética fundado en la experiencia histórica de las culturas americanas.* Buenos Aires: J. Roldán y Cía, 1924.

————. *La restauración nacionalista: crítica de la educación argentina y bases para una reforma en el estudio de las humanidades modernas.* 1909. Reprint. Buenos Aires: J. Roldán y Cía, 1922.

Romanell, Patrick. *Making of the Mexican Mind.* Notre Dame: University of Notre Dame Press, 1971.

Romero, José Luis. *Las ideas políticas en Argentina.* 5th ed. Buenos Aires: Fondo de Cultura Económica, 1981.

Romero, Sílvio. *História da literatura brasileira.* 2 vols. Rio de Janeiro: Garnier, 1888.

Roquette-Pinto, Edgar. *Ensaios de antropologia brasileira.* São Paulo: 1933.

————, ed. *Estudos afro-brasileiros.* Rio de Janeiro: Ed. Ariel, 1935.

————. *Seixos rolados.* Rio de Janeiro: Mendonça Machado, 1927.

Rosenblat, Angel. *La población indígena y el mestizaje en América.* 2 vols. Buenos Aires: Editorial Nova, 1954.

Saco, José Antonio. *Colección de papeles científicos, históricos, políticos y de otros ramos sobre la Isla de Cuba ya publicados, ya inéditos por don José Antonio Saco.* 3 vols. Havana: Editorial Lex, 1962.

Said, Edward W. *Orientalism.* New York: Pantheon Books, 1978.

Salvucci, Richard J. *Textiles and Capitalism in Mexico: An Economic History of the Obrajes, 1539–1840.* Princeton: Princeton University Press, 1987.

Sampaio, Antônio Gomes de Azevedo. *Abolicionismo: considerações gerais do movimento antiescravista e sua história limitada a Jacarehy, que foi um centro de acção no norte do estado de São Paulo*. São Paulo: n.p., 1890.

Sarmiento, Domingo F. *Condición del extranjero en América*. 2d ed. Buenos Aires: Librería "La Facultad," 1928.

————. *Conflicto y armonía de las razas en América (Conclusiones)*. Mexico City: Universidad Nacional Autónoma de México, 1978.

————. *Conflicto y armonías de las razas en América*. Buenos Aires: S. Ostwald Editor, 1883.

————. *Cuatro conferencias*. Buenos Aires: W. M. Jackson Editores, n.d.

Schwartz, Rosalie. "The Displaced and the Disappointed: Cultural Nationalists and Black Activists in Cuba in the 1920s." PhD diss., University of California, San Diego, 1977.

Schwartz, Stuart B. "Recent Trends in the Study of Slavery in Brazil."*Luso-Brazilian Review* 25, no. 1 (Summer 1988): 1–25.

Scobie, James R.*Argentina: A City and a Nation*. New York: Oxford University Press, 1964.

Scott, Rebecca J. *Slave Emancipation in Cuba: The Transition to Free Labor, 1860–1899*. Princeton, N.J.: Princeton University Press, 1985.

Serra, Rafael. *Ensayos políticos, sociales y económicos*. New York: Impr. A. W. Howes, 1899.

————.*Para blancos y negros. Ensayos políticos, sociales y económicos*. Havana: Imprenta "El Score," 1907.

Serviat, Pedro. *El problema negro en Cuba y su solución definitiva*. Havana: Empresa Poligráfica del CC del PCC, 1986.

Sierra, Justo. *The Political Evolution of the Mexican People*. Translated by Charles Ramsdell. Austin: University of Texas Press, 1969.

Simpson, Eyler N. *The Ejido: Mexico's Way Out*. Chapel Hill: University of North Carolina Press, 1937.

Sinkin, Richard. *The Mexican Reform, 1855–76: A Study in Liberal Nation-Building*. Austin: University of Texas Press, 1979.

Skidmore, Thomas E. *Black into White: Race and Nationality in Brazilian Thought*. New York: Oxford University Press, 1974.

————."Brazilian Intellectuals and the Problem of Race, 1870–1930." Occasional Paper No. 6 of the Graduate Center for Latin American Studies, Vanderbilt University, 1969.

————. "Gilberto Freyre and the Early Brazilian Republic: Some Notes on Methodology." *Comparative Studies in Society and History* 6, no. 4 (July 1964): 490–505.

————."Toward a Comparative Analysis of Race Relations Since Abolition in Brazil and the United States." *Journal of Latin American Studies* 4, pt. 1 (May 1972): 1–28.

Sofer, Eugene F. *From Pale to Pampa: A Social History of the Jews of Buenos Aires*. New York: Holmes & Meier, 1982.

Sola, José Sixto de. "Los extranjeros en Cuba." *Cuba Contemporánea* 8 (June 1915): 105–128.

————. "El pesimismo cubano." *Cuba Contemporánea* 3 (December 1913): 273–303.

Solberg, Carl. *Immigration and Nationalism: Argentina and Chile, 1890–1914*. Austin: University of Texas Press, 1970.

Sousa, João Cardoso Menezes e [Barão de Paranapiacaba]. *Teses sobre colonização do Brasil: projeto de solução as questões sociais que se prendem a este difícil problema*. Rio de Janeiro: Typ. Nacional, 1875.

Spencer, Herbert. *Essays, Scientific, Political and Speculative*. 3 vols. New York: Appleton, 1891.

————. *First Principles.* [? ed.] New York: Appleton, 1898.

————. *The Principles of Sociology.* 3 vols. New York: Appleton, 1889.

Stabb, Martin S. "Indigenism and Racism in Mexican Thought, 1857–1911." *Journal of Inter-American Studies* 1 (1959): 405–424.

————. *In Quest of Identity: Patterns in the Spanish American Essay of Ideas, 1890–1960.* Chapel Hill: University of North Carolina Press, 1967.

Starr, Frederick. *In Indian Mexico: A Narrative of Travel and Labor.* Chicago: Forbes & Co., 1908.

Stavenhagen, Rodolfo. *Las clases sociales en las sociedades agrarias.* Mexico: Siglo Veintiuno, 1971.

————. "México: minorías étnicas y política cultural." *Nexos* 19 (July 1979), 13–25.

Stepan, Nancy Leys. "Eugenics in Brazil, 1917–1940." In Mark Adams, ed., *New Directions in the History of Eugenics,* forthcoming.

————. *The Idea of Race in Science: Great Britain, 1800–1960.* London: Macmillan in association with St. Antony's College, Oxford, 1982.

Stocking, George. *Race, Culture and Evolution.* London: Collier-Macmillan, 1968.

Szuchman, Mark D. "The Limits of the Melting Pot in Urban Argentina: Marriage and Integration in Córdoba, 1869–1909." *Hispanic American Historical Review* 57, no. 1 (February 1977): 24–50.

Tannenbaum, Frank. *Slave and Citizen: The Negro in the Americas.* New York: Knopf, 1946.

Taylor, William. *Drink, Homicide and Rebellion in Colonial Mexican Villages.* Stanford: Stanford University Press, 1979.

Tejera, Diego Vicente. "Comentarios al proyecto de código criminal cubano." *Revista Bimestre Cubana* 21, no. 6 (November–December 1926): 846–862.

————. "El hondo problema de la pena de muerte." *Cuba Contemporánea* 42 (September–October 1926): 5–56.

Terán, Oscar. *Positivismo y nación en Argentina. Con una selección de textos de J. M. Ramos Mejía, A. Alvarez, C. O. Bunge y José Ingenieros.* Buenos Aires: Puntosur Editores, 1987.

Thomas, Hugh. *Cuba: The Pursuit of Freedom.* New York: Harper & Row, 1971.

Thompson, Ruth. "The Limitations of Ideology in the Early Argentine Labour Movement: Anarchism in the Trade Unions, 1890–1920." *Journal of Latin American Studies* 16, no. 1 (May 1984): 81–99.

Thorne, Christopher. *Allies of a Kind: The United States, Britain and the War against Japan, 1941–1945.* New York: Oxford University Press, 1978.

Toplin, Robert Brent. *The Abolition of Slavery in Brazil.* New York: Atheneum, 1972.

Torres, Alberto. *As fontes da vida no Brasil.* Rio de Janeiro: Imprensa Nacional, 1915.

————. *O problema nacional brasileiro.* Rio de Janeiro: Imprensa Nacional, 1914.

————. *Le problème mondial.* Rio de Janeiro: Imprensa Nacional, 1913.

Trelles, Carlos M. "El progreso y el retroceso de la República de Cuba." *Revista Bimestre Cubana* 18, no. 4 (July–August 1923): 313–319, and 18, no. 5 (September–October 1923): 345–364.

Ugarte, Manuel. *El destino de un continente.* Madrid: Editorial Mundo Latino, 1923.

————. *La patria grande.* Madrid: Editorial Internacional, 1924.

————. *El porvenir de la América Latina, la raza, la integridad territorial y moral, la organización interior.* Valencia: F. Sempere y Cía. Editores, n.d.

Van den Berghe, Pierre. *Race and Racism: A Comparative Perspective.* New York: Wiley, 1967.

Vanguardia, La (Buenos Aires), esp. 1918.

Vasconcelos, José. "The Latin-American Basis of Mexican Civilization." In José Vasconcelos and Manuel Gamio, *Aspects of Mexican Civilization*. Chicago: University of Chicago Press, 1926, 3–102.

———. *Memorias, Ulíses criollo, La tormenta*. Mexico: Fondo de Cultura Ecónomica, 1982.

———. *La raza cósmica, misión de la raza iberoamericana*. Paris: Agencia Mundial de Librería, 1925.

Vaughan, Mary Kay. *The State, Education and Social Class in Mexico, 1880–1928*. DeKalb: University of Northern Illinois Press, 1982.

Velasco, Carlos de. *Aspectos nacionales*. Havana: Jesús Montero, 1915.

———. "El problema negro." *Cuba Contemporánea* 1 (February 1913): 73–79.

———. "El problema religioso." *Cuba Contemporánea* 8 (July 1915): 209–223.

Venâncio Filho, Francisco. *Euclides da Cunha e seus amigos*. São Paulo: Ed. Nacional, 1938.

Veríssimo, José. Review in *Jornal do Comércio* (Rio de Janeiro, December 4, 1889).

Vianna, F. J. Oliveira. *Populações meridionais do Brasil*. 2 vols., 5th ed. São Paulo: José Olympio, 1952.

———. "O povo brasileiro e sua evolução." In Ministério da Agricultura, Indústria e Commercio, Directoria Geral de Estatística, *Recenseamento do Brasil realizado em 1 de Setembro de 1920*, vol. 1: *Introducção*. Rio de Janeiro, 1922, 279–400.

Villoldo, Julio. "El lynchamiento, social y jurídicamente considerado." *Cuba Contemporánea* 21 (September 1919): 5–19.

Walter, Richard J. *The Socialist Party of Argentina, 1890–1930*. Austin: University of Texas Press, 1972.

Williams, Glyn. "Welsh Settlers and Native Americans in Patagonia." *Journal of Latin American Studies* 11, no. 1 (May 1979): 41–66.

Womack, John. *Zapata and the Mexican Revolution*. New York: Vintage Books, 1969.

Woodward, Ralph Lee, Jr., ed. *Positivism in Latin America, 1850–1900: Are Order and Progress Reconcilable?* Lexington, Mass.: Heath, 1971.

Zeballos, Estanislao S. *Descripción amena de la República Argentina*. 2 vols. Buenos Aires: Imprenta J. Peuser, 1881.

Zum Felde, Alberto. *Indice crítico de la literatura hispanoamericana*. 2 vols. Mexico City: Editorial Guarania, 1954.

Index